The Perfect Brand Job

How to Grow Your Business Fast and Enjoy a Happy Exit Strategy

EDWARD J. BALDEGA

© Copyright 2022 - All rights reserved.

The content contained within this book may not be reproduced, duplicated or transmitted without direct written permission from the author or the publisher.

Under no circumstances will any blame or legal responsibility be held against the publisher, or author, for any damages, reparation, or monetary loss due to the information contained within this book, either directly or indirectly.

Legal Notice:

This book is copyright protected. It is only for personal use. You cannot amend, distribute, sell, use, quote or paraphrase any part, or the content within this book, without the consent of the author or publisher.

Disclaimer Notice:

Please note the information contained within this document is for educational and entertainment purposes only. All effort has been executed to present accurate, up to date, reliable, complete information. No warranties of any kind are declared or implied. Readers acknowledge that the author is not engaged in the rendering of legal, financial, medical or professional advice. The content within this book has been derived from various sources. Please consult a licensed professional before attempting any techniques outlined in this book.

By reading this document, the reader agrees that under no circumstances is the author responsible for any losses, direct or indirect, that are incurred as a result of the use of the information contained within this document, including, but not limited to, errors, omissions, or inaccuracies.

TABLE OF CONTENTS

INTRODUCTION — v
    Your Brand

PART ONE
GROWING YOUR BUSINESS

CHAPTER 1 — 3
Know What Makes You Different
    Solve a Problem — 4
        Step One of Problem Solving: How Do I Solve This Problem? — 4
        Step Two of Problem Solving: Is This a Shared Problem? — 5
    Note Your Purpose — 6
    Know Your Why — 8

CHAPTER 2 — 11
Have a Clear Mission Statement
    Know Your Value — 13

CHAPTER 3 — 15
Your Target Audience
    Can You Niche Down? — 17

CHAPTER 4 — 19
A Unique Brand Logo

CHAPTER 5 — 23
Create Your Brand Story
    Turn Your Purpose Into Something Actionable — 25
    Use Your Voice and Introduce Yourself — 27
    Emotional Connection — 27

CHAPTER 6 — 31
From Letterhead to Website

Chapter 7   35
Know the Competition
  Follow the Competition's Example   38
  Learn From Their Mistakes   39

Chapter 8   41
Communication is Key
  Find Your Voice   44

Chapter 9   47
The Tools for Building a Brand
  Resources   48
    Communities   48
  Tools and Services   48
    Website Tools   50
    Editing Tools   51
    Marketing Tools   51
    Analytics Tools   52

PART TWO
SELLING YOUR BUSINESS

Chapter 1   57
Figuring Out Your Exit Style
  Understand the Options   59
    Selling   59
    Mergers & Acquisitions   61
    IPO (Initial Public Offering)   63
    Liquidation or Closing   66

Chapter 2   69
Getting Your Ducks in a Row
  Legal   69
    Letters of Intent   70
    Purchase and Sale Agreement   70
    Non-Compete Agreements   71

    Earn-Out Agreements   72
    Seller Financing Agreements   73
  Financial   73
  Marketing   75
  Within the Brand   76
    Talk to Your Investors   77
    Talk to Employees   77
    Tell Customers   78

Chapter 3   79
Determining the Sale Price
  Getting a Professional Valuation   80
  How to Value the Company   81

Chapter 4   83
Documents
  Client Lists   83
    Finances   84
    Business Operations   84
    Product/Services   84
    Clients (Customers) and Suppliers/Distributors   84
    Brand Specific   85
    Equipment and Building   85
    Employees   85

Chapter 5   87
How to Sell
  Word of Mouth   87
  Business Broker   88
  Web-Based Business Seller   89

Chapter 6   91
Getting the Word Out
  Timing   91
  Tell It Like It Is   92
  Next   92

And Then	93
The Legal Side Of It	93
The Clients Might Be Getting Suspicious	94

Chapter 7
Putting Taxes in Order — 95

File Final Taxes and Related Forms	96
Sole Proprietorship	96
Partnership	96
Corporations	97
Don't Forget Your Employees	97
Employment Taxes	98
Pension or Benefit Plans	98
Pay Your Taxes	99
Report Payments to Contractors	99
Cancel Your EIN, Close Your IRS Business Account	99
Keep Your Paperwork	100
In Summary of Your Taxes	100

Chapter 8
Mistakes to Avoid — 101

Valuation is Too High	102
Trying to Do it Alone	103
Failing to Plan Ahead	104
Inflexibility	105
Your Heart's Not In It	106

Conclusion — 107

Growing Your Business	107
Selling Your Business	108

References — 111

INTRODUCTION

If you don't think you have the nerve to build a business, stop reading this book. Building a business is scary, if not overwhelming, so you will need nerves of steel to do it.

Seriously, starting a business can sometimes be scary and very stressful. However, you can ease the pressure by breaking it into steps. Focus on one thing at a time to make your life much easier.

This book will help you understand what it takes to start and run a successful business by breaking down each step. Too much information can lead to confusion and an overwhelming urge to give up. That's where this book comes in.

The first chapter will show you what it means to build your brand. A successful brand is a business that is more than just making money. Next, you'll start to understand the basics of what it takes to start your business. Each chapter builds on that first one, showing you how to take one thought and naturally progress to the next strategy involved.

From developing a strong mission statement to researching the competition, I will explain everything you need to know to build a solid brand. But then I will show you how to sell that brand with a smooth transition.

In fact, this book is two parts; Part 1 is all about building a business. Part 2 is about selling that business. So, you're getting a lot of bang for your buck when you start reading this book. Of course, there are books about building a business and separate books about selling a business, but this one covers both! Because let's face it, you will inevitably want to sell a business after building it. Whether it's to retire or start flipping companies, that day will come.

YOUR BRAND

A business's brand is how your company is recognized. What is your business recognized for? It is not to be confused with your logo or slogan; those are marketing tools. No, your brand is a concept. The thing that determines what people say, think, or feel about your business.

Within this book, I will discuss a purpose-driven brand. As humans, we are driven by purpose. You know, the meaning of life kind of thing. Why are we here, and how can we make this world a better place? If, as individuals, we feel that we must live our lives to our fullest potential, then businesses should follow the same guidelines. The Oxford Dictionary says that the definition of purpose is "The reason for which something is done or created or for which something exists." Our sense of purpose, or the reason we exist, drives our likes and dislikes.

For example, if our purpose is to pay attention to what the planet needs to continue supporting human life, it would be against that purpose to do business with a company that blindly pollutes and contaminates this world. Therefore, if a company's target audience wants solutions to pollution or contamination, I will see that my company follows suit as a business owner.

Done correctly, your brand will be your company's most valuable asset. It's your reputation; a good reputation can be worth millions in business.

You will need to keep three things clear while building your brand. First, people will always be skeptical of a purpose-driven brand. When the end goal of your business is to make money, everything you do becomes suspect in the eyes of the public. Even if your company addresses a cause, the public views it as a smoke screen, a ruse.

Some simply mix up terms, confusing your purpose, vision, and mission. So, let's break them down so you can commit them to memory. Because when you know the why, what, and where, you can overcome the negative and focus on your cause.

Purpose—your why: Other than to make money, why do you do what you do?

Vision—your where: Where do you want your brand to go? What does the future of your brand look like?

Mission—your what: To reach your vision, what are you committed to doing?

People trust brands they know. A product with a good brand will fetch a higher price, and the customer is willing to pay that price. Why? Because the brand has an excellent reputation and has created that sense of trust. The trust says:

- this product is high quality.
- this product lasts forever.
- this product tastes the best.
- this product is beautiful.

… the bottom line:

- this product is worth every penny.

That's the kind of brand I want to help you build for your business. I want to see you take your business idea and turn it into a brand that will have customers banging on your door for your services.

Part One
Growing Your Business

Chapter 1

KNOW WHAT MAKES YOU DIFFERENT

You must distinguish what makes you different from all the companies like yours. For example, you've decided to open a bookstore. There are many bookstores, so what's going to set yours apart? What will you do that is different from the rest? Is it what you do or how you do it that's different? Are your hours what sets you apart? Are you a bookstore that caters to the night owls, the insomniacs, or that person who needs a book to read during their graveyard shift? Whatever it is, you need to know it; then, you need to capitalize on it. Choose the one thing that sets you apart, then focus on it.

This chapter will help you with more than the *what*, though. First, I'll explain what a brand is. Then I'll go over the reasons for developing a purpose-driven brand. Then I'll talk about the Golden Circle, as described by Simon Sinek in his TED Talk and his book, *Start With Why*. There are three aspects to creating your brand that you need to understand. Two are the easiest to recognize. First, you know what you do and probably know how you do it. That is where what makes you different comes in.

You sell books is the what, but the how is that special something that sets you apart from everyone else?

But the last, most vital part of that Golden Circle is the *why*; this chapter will explain that to you.

SOLVE A PROBLEM

You're probably thinking to yourself; *I've solved the problem that I think so many people have when it comes to books.* You're going to open a bookstore that caters to late-night shoppers, and maybe you're even going to set up a few areas in that bookstore where people can sit with a book and read. Maybe, you think, *they can rent the book for an hour or two and just read.* Perhaps they don't want to buy the book and don't want take it home, and risk misplacing it, so they just rent it and read it right there. *That's a pretty cool idea*, you figure. And you're right; it's a novel idea.

Step One of Problem Solving: How Do I Solve This Problem?

So, you've tackled one of the most critical steps of starting a business. You've solved the problem for, hopefully, a large enough percentage of the population. Maybe you've figured this out because you took an overnight trip to a new city and found yourself unable to sleep in your hotel room with nothing to read. You got antsy. But you didn't know where to go, and you certainly didn't know where you could buy a book. And a book is just one more thing to pack in your suitcase, so that would be a waste of money. Although a late-night bookstore—someplace to rent a book for a couple of hours—that's something to consider.

Now that you're excited because you've found your niche—the *what* of your business—you realize you've never heard people talking about this problem before. So you worry, and the idea of even being able to "sell" your midnight bookstore slash book rental place starts running through your mind.

Step Two of Problem Solving: Is This a Shared Problem?

It might feel weird to talk to people about your idea because, really, how many people will go for it? Will they look at you like you suddenly sprouted a second head, or will they open up and admit they've run into the same problem? This would be a good time to Google what you figure is the problem. Maybe search for "is there a bookstore open at midnight near me?" or something along those lines. Doing this will tell you if it's something that others have searched for or if you're alone in this adventure.

Now it's getting exciting! You've Googled and found that people look for midnight bookstores, and you figure you can bring even more people in when they find out you offer the option just to rent a book rather than sell them. You can even Google "rent a book" and find out what that option looks like.

In this step, you'll want to reach out to people via email, your website, or whatever platform you have available. Marketing your upcoming business is going to be an essential step. But remember, when you start promoting or marketing, don't scare your potential customers.

Naturally, you'll want to talk about your experiences looking for a bookstore in the middle of the night. Still, you don't want to frighten people by painting all the awful sleepless nights, wishing you had a book, a comfortable chair to lounge in while drinking some tea, and reading a good book. Instead, you want to let them know that they have a need, you understand that need, and you're going to fill that need.

So rather than focusing on the problem—not having a book in the middle of the night when you can't sleep and you're pacing the apartment with nothing to do—instead focus on the solution—curling up in a comfy chair in a relaxing environment with a cup of hot cocoa or tea and a good book.

Another aspect of this part of problem-solving is that you can get feedback from potential customers. For example, what are they looking for in a midnight bookstore? How are their needs the same yet different from yours, and how can you solve all their problems, rather than just one?

NOTE YOUR PURPOSE

Your purpose is probably the most vital information you need to start your business and set up your brand. First, remember that your purpose should not be to make money or become famous. Money and fame are simply a result of the business and should not be considered your purpose. Of course, you want to make money; everyone does. But what is the deeper reason? What drives you, motivates you, makes you get out of bed in the morning? What is the drive behind your brand, or should I say, what is your dream?

Just wanting to provide someone a place to read a book at midnight isn't the dream, is it? Because there is probably more to it than that. Does it have to do with a sense of belonging? Is it a desire to give everyone a place to feel welcome, no matter the time of day or night? Bottom line, does sitting in a bookstore at midnight answer some deep-seated need within yourself that you know resonates with others?

When trying to solidify your purpose, take a moment to reflect on real-world issues that resonate with you. Authenticity is the key to your purpose, so it should have meaning. Therefore, you'll "find" your why or purpose rather than "choose" or "strategize." This purpose must come from your soul.

Start with research. Figure out what your target customers consider the biggest problems that need attention, and if one of those is on your list, then you're on your way. But remember, don't choose a cause just because it's got the highest percentage rate of customers who consider it an issue that needs to be solved. Customers can spot a fake right out of the gate, and many companies have been made aware that gaining ground after a major faux pas is one of the most challenging things to do.

Let's look at the history of brands and their purpose. Company brands didn't always have a purpose unless you count making tons of money and becoming rich and famous. Brands used to determine the rules and largely ignored consumers. But then, the digital revolution rolled around, and internet chat rooms gave consumers a voice. They used that voice and began to vocalize their opinions. Loudly and in great numbers.

Companies were forced to pay attention to what their customers wanted. Then, with customers recognizing their own purpose and place in the world, businesses realized they needed to do the same or lose money. Customers wanted to do business with companies that shared their values. So began the purpose behind a brand, something more than just the desire for money or fame.

Brands realized their customers cared about the ethics and morals of the companies they did business with. Customers wanted to do business with brands that cared and didn't plan on letting these big companies get away with their typical unethical practices or sloppy customer service.

All of this leads to the *why* of your business. First, you must know why you want to begin a business, to start a brand. And it must have a deeper meaning than fame and fortune. Let those things be a natural byproduct of your brand, but focus on what you can do for the world. What changes can you make on this planet to improve it for everyone?

That's something to think about as you read this book and is the first, most crucial step toward building your brand. Let's clarify the steps you must take to find your purpose. I will discuss some of these steps in the next section of this chapter.

1. Focus on your cause
2. Determine your *why*
3. Know your customer's *why*
4. Analyze your *why*

To help you understand steps 2 through 4, I have some great words of wisdom from someone who knows what he's talking about when it comes to a brand purpose, and we will go over those in the next section of this chapter.

KNOW YOUR WHY

According to Simon Sinek's Golden Circle, the *why* is at the center of building your brand. It's the key to it all, as explained about understanding your purpose. So your purpose is your *why*. Now, without sounding like I'm telling you what to do, your *why* is probably not because you want everyone to be able to read a book whenever they want. That is a good reason, but you need to know the specifics of why you want that.

Why would it be important to you that everyone has access to a good book, even in the middle of the night? Knowing your *why* will help you in three areas of your business:
- The ability to stand up for some belief that will add value to the lives of others.
- The ability to stand out in a large group of booksellers.
- The ability to stand firm with a company culture that will show longevity and a clear goal for its company.

Not everyone knows their *why*, and some probably don't care. But when you start with the *why*, you're motivated by the right thing. Instead of pursuing wealth and fame, you'll be on the quest for a dream. Knowing your *why* will set the stage for a reliable and longtime customer base because your priorities will match theirs, and you will gain their trust.

Knowing your customer's *why* is the same as yours is part of step 3. For example, we all have a dream, a vision of how we think the world should be, but it doesn't always match up to someone else's dream. This is important because you won't have brand loyalty or customers if you can't align your *why* with theirs. I mentioned earlier that you need to know your customers. Again, if customers can't trust that you understand them, they won't be interested in what you have to offer. So, no matter how charitable your *why* is, it won't matter if your customers don't buy into it.

But now, let's talk about the three things your *why* will do for your business.

1. When you have a belief that you're willing to stand up for, you can change lives. No matter how many people come into your bookstore, all it takes is one person whose *why* matches yours to bring fulfillment and satisfaction.
2. When you think about it, every bookstore is the same, offering books, to coffee, to scones. But following your *why* can set you apart, make you stand out from the others, and be noticed. And okay, most people who go to bookstores just want a book and probably even a coffee. However, you don't want to leave anyone out; therefore, being different will help find those people, the insomniacs and night owls, who need what you have to offer in your bookstore.
3. A company built with a clear vision of your goals is a company with a long-term mission. Longevity comes because it's always going to be a company that fulfills dreams. You want to sell to people who believe what you believe. On top of that, if you hire employees who share your vision, they will work for more than just a paycheck. They will give their heart and soul to their job to keep your dream alive.

Once you've figured out your *why* and aligned it with your customer's, you need to analyze it. In other words, put everything together and see if it all lines up. To figure this out, there are some questions that you need to ask yourself.

- Does my purpose contribute to society or the environment positively?
- Who benefits from my contribution to this cause?
- Does my business have a direct connection to the cause?
- Have my customers shown concern for this cause?
- Does the public agree that I am qualified to address this problem?
- Is my leadership team emotionally invested in this cause?

- Will they do everything possible within the company to help this cause?

The answers to these questions must be positive to confirm that your business is qualified and can address the problem at hand. The general public should believe that you have the right to weigh in on the matter.

So, know your *why* because it's the heart of your business.

Chapter 2

HAVE A CLEAR MISSION STATEMENT

Once you've found your *why*, you must make sure you have a clear mission statement—something every business should have. Let the world know what your company does, and more importantly, why. See, there's that *why* again. The mission statement is a brief explanation of your dream, and by having one, your midnight bookstore will reach out to those that understand your *why*.

A mission statement should reach people outside the parameters of the customer you're targeting. For example, maybe someone is looking to find out why a bookstore would be open at midnight. Perhaps they've never experienced that need to find a book in the middle of the night. But something you've said in your mission statement reaches them deeper. You've inspired them, and they realize your business is something they can get behind.

Never underestimate the power of your vision.

Remember, you have a story to tell, and it's probably a long story. However, your mission statement needs to be concise and to the point, and it needs to be memorable. You need to get to the heart of the matter when it comes to your story. So, first, capture your customers' interest in one to three sentences. Then, put your sentences together using just the right parts of speech. Verbs, adverbs, nouns, and adjectives that paint a picture are the keys to making your mission statement one that will capture attention while getting your story across quickly and vividly.

Keep in mind, though, that your mission statement may change over time. Sometimes, as your business grows, your goals change. Maybe your dream gets adjusted a little. So take the time to review your mission statement regularly and update it as needed. Your mission statement does not need to be set in stone.

The following are reasons for putting together a mission statement:

- Guiding light: The mission statement shows your employees the path to follow as they navigate their work with your business. Knowing what drives a company can offer stability while increasing motivation and productivity.
- Explains the *why*: Your mission statement is another way to describe the *why* behind your business. Remember, there is more to a business than just making money or becoming famous. Your mission statement explains the value behind your company, and your value is what you can do for others by offering the services your business entails.
- Foundation for marketing: Your mission statement is also helpful to your marketing team. Before you market your company, you must keep your mission statement in mind. When you fully understand what you do, you will be better able to market your business to reach your target audience.
- Brand loyalty: Your mission statement will allow potential customers to find you. Once they have found your company, they will offer unwavering support through brand loyalty. In other words, they will consistently purchase from you and may even bring in additional customers.

Part of understanding your *why* is to understand your company's value to the world. So when thinking of your mission statement, remember it is the *what* of your company. Therefore, you need to let your target audience know the *why* and *what* you plan on doing to reach your vision.

Remember this quote from Tiffany from *How to Entrepreneur* and the article, "*What is a Business Brand? Your Answer Revealed…*"

"Don't just write a mission, be on a mission!" (Tiffany, 2018).

KNOW YOUR VALUE

Your principles and values will further the progress of your business. When you list your values, remember to keep them limited so people can easily remember them. Generally, your values will begin with verbs like "Be committed," and "Deliver excellence."

Your company's values will consist of ethical principles or behavior standards. These values will be highly critical to your company's success. If you already have a team lined up, have them brainstorm ideas with you.

However, because it's your vision—your dream—you will know what ethical practices you want within the business. Your vision will represent your most sacred value to the world, your employees, and your customers. Your brand's values should also be inspirational rather than transactional.

- Transactional: Focuses on the task of selling books to people late at night.
- Inspirational: Focuses on the people, inspiring them to make a difference—customers become family, and we welcome them into a place of comfort and acceptance.

If your values begin to feel more transactional, question the behaviors and principles of your company. This examination will help you adjust your company's values to align with your vision and dream. Never let someone else's values or principles affect what your company does. Everyone within your company should reflect your principles. Remember, everyone within your company is a reflection of your Why, and it needs to stay that way.

Remember, your values should move the company forward in its progress. Sometimes the values will adapt as the most current competitive environment warrants. However, they should stay aligned with your values that drive the *why* of your company.

As an inspiration, your company will have the potential for greatness. Your company can move the world forward by utilizing inspirational values. Challenge the world's idea of what a bookstore should look like, then merge that vision with a strategy that will increase your company's potential and success.

Chapter 3

YOUR TARGET AUDIENCE

A target audience is precisely what it sounds like. Any business is explicitly created to service a specific group of people. Sometimes you have a broad target audience, but once in a while, you narrow that focus to a smaller group. Naturally, you would think that the larger your target audience, the better your potential for success, because the odds are in your favor. However, it's the opposite. It works in your favor to thin out your target audience. You just upped your game when your target audience is smaller, because your values are inspirational enough to shake up the world's perception of what your business should look like. You're changing the world one customer at a time, and if done right, that audience will grow as your success increases.

But first, you must consider specific factors when determining your target audience.
- age
- gender
- location
- education
- socioeconomic status

Of course, sometimes you will need to be more specific in your specifications of a target audience, because as the world changes, so must your marketing tactics.

You must figure out your target audience to create a successful marketing strategy. No matter how many people you want to reach, you don't want to spend money advertising to the ones who aren't interested in your company. And it's not even that they're not interested; there are just some people who will not want or need your product.

For instance, you don't want to try to market your midnight bookstore to people who live in rural areas where there is no bookstore for miles. Likewise, you're not going to advertise to people under a certain age, because there are probably no ten-year-olds who will be coming into your store in the middle of the night.

Be as specific as possible when figuring out the demographics of your target audience. Narrowing down the qualifications allows you to put together the best marketing strategy. Don't think of it as limiting when you begin to narrow your search, though. For example, your midnight bookstore is filling a need, and that need is pretty narrow, but it's not quite the niche market that you might fear it is. However, we will discuss these niche markets in the next section. For now, though, recognize that you must narrow the parameters of your ideal target audience.

To successfully market your business, you need to create a direct connection with your audience, which can only happen when you have the specifics of your target audience. For instance, you would not pitch an idea the same way to more than one gender or age group. Likewise, you would not launch an idea in the same way to different religions. You need to keep this in mind when you decide on your target audience because you will approach the idea of a midnight bookstore in various ways.

When you determine your target audience, remember that your goal is to earn the audience's trust. Establishing this trust comes from making a personal connection and striking a chord with your target audience. You need to know more about your customers to build this trust.

One criticism that comes up when talking about your target audience, is the potential to overlook possible customers. You may be so focused on the people you think will want your services that you forget the outliers—the potential people that would surprise you as a customer but could be a solid part of the brand loyalty you're looking for.

So keep in mind while you're narrowing down your target audience, that it's sometimes easy to overlook a group of people that should be included. But it's also important to note that you should consistently take the time to go back over your target audience as your business grows. You may find that some parameters change or expand to include others as your business changes. But if you stay true to your vision, the changes will only be for the best. I mean, it's not a bad thing to add to your customer base.

CAN YOU NICHE DOWN?

I mentioned earlier that you might worry that your niche market is too narrow. However, that isn't a bad thing. You can niche down if you realize that the target audience you're looking at is too broad and that you won't be able to market your services successfully.

At first, the idea of niching down might be scary. You've heard you will not make money if your niche market is too small. But remember that your ultimate goal will never be the amount you earn. Yes, you hope that would always be a good side effect of your business, but you can't let that alone drive you.

You have a vision, a world-changing reason for your business. The money-making part of it is the product of your midnight bookstore. So you need to step back and consider your target audience. Do you include people because you're scared to leave anyone out? Are you ticking off boxes because you want to help everyone, and it just kills you to think you might miss someone—so you spend an agonizing amount of time convincing yourself of all the reasons they would be interested?

I say, niche down. Especially since you're starting a bookstore business in a market full of bookstores; how do you compete? I mentioned earlier that you need to stand out. So not only does your vision need to make you stand out, but you need to stand out by offering something so unique that it narrows your target audience even more.

But don't panic; remember I said that narrowing your target audience does not have to be scary, and it's a good thing. So let me list why niching down is the best way to grow your business and succeed.

- **You'll find your specific audience:** When you niche down, you will narrow your target audience until you reach the core of what you're looking for. You'll find the people who will build your loyal customers and show true brand loyalty. Next, you want to impact your customers, which is how you will do it. Then, when you market your business, it'll be like you're talking directly to the customers you're looking for.
- **You'll develop a relationship with your customers:** When you market to your niched down target audience, they will know that you are talking to them. You'll make them feel special, and this will also help them believe that you understand them. You know them, and you want to help them.
- **You'll be an expert at a specific thing:** It's more comfortable for a customer to do business with someone good at something. It gives them trust in the service you're offering. You offer what so many others do, but you're unique. You're an expert at selling books in the middle of the night, and if that's what your customers want, then they've come to the right place.

Let's think about the idea of niching down. Once you've figured out who your target audience will be, ensure they're willing to pay you for it. But also, remember that you might niche down a little more once you've talked to potential customers on Reddit or other platforms. Get some informal yet valuable feedback.

Remember, your goal is to know your customers, so you need to go where they are. Then, to find that target audience and figure out what they want. Only then will you be able to niche down to where you need to be with your brand.

Chapter 4

A UNIQUE BRAND LOGO

One of the most effective tools in your marketing strategy is your brand logo. Your logo will be your company's face; the first thing people see about your business. Not only is it an image, but it's also a point of recognition. Consider it your brand's foundation.

Often, a customer will make a split-second decision about a company. Therefore, a good logo is the best way to make that decision positive. In addition, your logo should assure the customer that your company is professional, trustworthy, and provides excellent customer service.

So, let's talk about the critical elements of a brand logo:

- **attention-grabber:** Your brand has about two seconds to convince customers that your service is worth their time and money.
- **first impression:** As I mentioned, your logo sets the tone of your brand. A good logo that interests customers will draw them in.
- **brand identity:** The foundation of your brand identity will be set within your logo. The colors, tones, and fonts tell a story. Then, your marketing team will take some of the best features of your logo and implement them into all company material—business cards, websites, letterheads, etc.
- **memorable:** Your logo should be so memorable in its visual aspect that customers will easily recognize your product and

business. It's like seeing the logo of your favorite or least favorite car manufacturer. If you're a Ford person, seeing that logo makes you happy. And, of course, if you spot the symbol of a car you don't like, you'll probably feel on edge. So it makes sense that you'll want your brand logo recognizable for being a top-notch business.
- **sets you apart:** Your logo should represent your business's unique, distinctive parts. You've set yourself apart from all the rest of the bookstores, so let it show in your logo. So you're a midnight bookstore—maybe the moon and stars should be a part of your logo. Think of it like that.
- **brand loyalty:** As your business grows, customers will begin recognizing your logo. As this recognition increases and customers become familiar with your business practices, your logo will become a source of trust. People will buy from you because they know they can trust your company.
- **emotional responses:** Colors represent emotions, so pay attention to the color scheme of your logo. If your goal is to evoke a sense of peace or calm, you'll stay away from vibrant colors like red. Do some research to determine the emotions that each color can bring about.
- **reflection of the business:** Some logos can showcase the company they represent. Nike is the best example of this. Nike is the Greek goddess of victory, so the swoosh logo that Nike has created represents speed; one of the qualities that someone might need to attain victory. Think of this while designing your logo.

So overall, the factors that come into play when designing your logo would be:
- distinctive
- unique
- memorable
- impactful

- detailed
- consistent styles
- imagery

The bottom line for your logo is that it needs to represent your business. Think of all the logos you've seen and the images and impressions they give you. Then consider what your business will offer and what you want people to think of when they see your logo. One thing I will always come back to when talking about making a decision is research. If an idea is not coming readily to you, it's time to research some of your thoughts. Start typing in some of the one-word ideas you've been jotting down. Ask around, as well, and find out what appeals to people. Sketch some ideas, then do a few surveys to see if you're headed in the right direction. Inspiration will hit, of that, I am sure.

Chapter 5

CREATE YOUR BRAND STORY

Every brand has a story. Every business has a beginning and a reason for that beginning. You need to figure out yours. Naturally, you have a story, a reason behind opening these midnight bookstores. For your target audience to want to visit your store, they need to feel that your story is their story.

But you must follow a few steps before you can get that story told. This is the beginning of the consistency I'll be talking about in this chapter, which I've mentioned a few times before in previous chapters. Your goal here is to put together the perfect plan and tell your story so that you cement your place in the hearts of your target audience. You will successfully edge out every competitor.

Let's look at Nike again. Of course, that swoosh logo has nothing to do with the company's name. But Nike told their story so that a simple check mark became "a million-dollar Swoosh," (Javed, 2020).

But let me explain a little better. First, I just wanted to let you know that the connection you feel to Nike when you see their swoosh is from neural coupling. In his article *"Brand Essentials—How to Create an Authentic Brand Story"* Faisal Javed explains this phenomenon in detail.

He writes that a story is what creates a connection with your target audience. Neural coupling is the human brain's reaction to the power of stories. These connections influence our sensory and motor cortex, creating the experience we feel when listening to a story. This experience then builds a connection to the storyteller. The neural coupling happens because the storyteller and the listener mirror each other's feelings through deeper understanding and comprehension.

The bottom line is that we are 22 times more likely to remember a story than a plain fact. Therefore, when you put your story together, remember these critical elements:

1. State the problem: As I've mentioned before, your story should state the problem that you want to help solve. This is whatever cause you have chosen to fight for, and it's your *why*.
2. Own your underdog status: You can join the ranks of the companies that have taken up a cause because their founder has been an underdog; someone who figured out how to solve the problem they shared with millions of people.
3. Revisit your experience: No matter how often the problem you're trying to solve has been addressed, your specific story still needs to be told. Especially since you may have a unique way of approaching the cause, which can be the impetus your target audience needs to support your endeavors.
4. Connect with your target audience: Your brand will connect on a deeper level with your customers when you tell your story. When you're successful, your brand becomes integral to your target audience's life.
5. Stay active in your cause: As your business's founder, you must always stay active in the cause and business. It's your story, so you don't want people to think you don't believe in your story anymore. Therefore, you need to stay in front of the business.

6. Know who you are and what you do: Always remember your purpose and *why*. It's when you forget that things can unravel.
7. Do good: Continue to do the good that you started doing. Remember, customers have long memories, and you cannot suddenly abandon your cause if you want to stay successful in your business.

When you address all these elements in your brand story, you will have succeeded in setting up a successful brand. A successful brand makes a successful business, and as long as you meet the above elements, your brand will continue to succeed.

TURN YOUR PURPOSE INTO SOMETHING ACTIONABLE

You've figured out the cause you want to follow with your brand, and you know why. But to get to that *why* with your customers, you must plan it out. You cannot go into this sounding vague, or like it was an idea you just rolled out when you hopped out of bed this morning. Research comes in handy right now, of course.

Find out details of the broad issue surrounding the cause you will tackle. You need to know what is already being done, who's doing it, and if there is an organization that would benefit from you joining forces with them.

Then, and here's a vital piece of information: look for gaps. Is there a way to address this cause from a different angle? Do you have the ability to offer something that others haven't thought of or that nobody else does? Once you've made that connection, you need to put together the details of your plan.

- What will you do?
- How will you do it?
- What resources will you use? Your resources can range from product to time to special skills.
- Will you focus on the cause with education, studies, or conversation?

- Will your contribution be physical, digital, or both?

No plan is complete until you set goals. You can have the best strategy in the world, but if you don't have goals, that plan can end up all over the place and never come to fruition.

- What are the goals?
- What is our timeline to achieve these goals?
- How are we going to measure these goals?

Measuring your achievements seems like a strange goal, but it's probably the most important. First, you need to be able to determine if what you're doing is working. If it's not and you haven't seen any response to your actions, then it's time to figure out another plan. And I don't mean a response like money being made. Have you seen an improvement in whatever cause you've taken up? Do you see a change? You may need to be realistic about this part and recognize that it may take some time for a change to take effect.

Within this goal, measuring is the idea of going public with it. I can't stress enough the importance of transparency in your goals and your journey with this cause. Being transparent and letting the public know your progress will also hold you accountable for your actions, which helps keep you on track. You don't want to lose sight of the cause; sometimes, making money can blind you to the original purpose.

This is not to say that making money is wrong because it's not, and honestly, it's the result of every business I know of unless you're a non-profit. It's just that while you're making money, you need to keep sight of your goal and your cause. If your plan is actionable and you hold yourself accountable with consistent public reporting, your purpose will have more substance than just a printed idea.

A quick thought while thinking about setting your goals. The timeline you want to put together should include short, medium, and long-term goals. Put together a calendar of your analysis and reporting that you will do, as well. Again, holding yourself accountable for your actions is something we should all do to stay on track. It's easy to put off doing what we know we should if we aren't being held accountable to anyone for it.

USE YOUR VOICE AND INTRODUCE YOURSELF

Your brand purpose statement will be your short statement that answers the questions:
- Why you do what you do.
- What you're committed to doing to reach your future vision.

Some brands use their purpose statement as their mission statement. Just remember that it needs to answer both of those questions above. Like your mission statement, it needs to be memorable enough for staff to remember it so they can live by it. The cause you have chosen should be at its core. It should inspire everyone from your leadership team to the public.

That sounds like a daunting task, to write a statement that inspires everyone from your employees to the general public. But remember that when you have a purpose, that vision can be the inspiration you need to write this statement and then follow it up with your story.

EMOTIONAL CONNECTION

You will make an emotional connection to your target audience with your story. Remember when you were a kid and story time was your favorite part of the day? Whether at school or home, that emotional contentment you felt when listening to a story was the best feeling in the world. We don't lose that emotional connection when we become adults; we just don't have the opportunity to listen to stories. But that's why movies and videos interest us so much. It's a form of storytelling, and we love it.

You have the opportunity to get that emotional connection, the neural coupling, with the public. Whether it's your target audience or anyone who's stumbled across your story, this emotional connection will create the goodwill you need to attract customers. That includes customers who are not in your target audience. If a customer is not part of your target audience, your brand story will make them want to take a chance with you.

Of course, while telling your story, you don't need to be telling a new one. Often, the emotional appeal is when you couldn't find something you needed, so you created it for yourself. And I can't say it enough, but people will not build that emotional attachment to a brand with the purpose of making money. They already know that a business should make a profit, so they want to see what you'll do with some of that money. Or how your service or product can benefit the world.

Refine your story.

There may be distracting elements that will cause a customer to lose interest.

Get to the point.

You will create many drafts of your story since no first draft is perfect. Share it with someone who hasn't heard it, then get feedback. Is there too much information? Is there not enough?

People don't connect with things; they connect with people. Therefore, using the hero's journey as a guide or template while telling your story is a good idea. Inspired by mythology, the hero's journey is a popular storytelling structure that shows the challenges a hero faces while trying to achieve a goal. Here are the basic steps for the hero's journey:

1. The protagonist, or hero, lives an ordinary life until there is a call to adventure.
    a. call to adventure: the problem that inspired your business—no book to read when awake at midnight.
2. The hero begins the journey but runs into difficulties.
    a. difficulties: no open bookstores at midnight.
3. The hero achieves the goal and returns home triumphant and transformed.

So in your story, you need to share the journey and its results. Then, within it, you'll answer the following questions:
- Did you start your business?
- How were you personally affected?
- What is the effect on your community and customers?

Remember, every part of your brand should:
- be consistent.
- have a purpose.
- be authentic.

This includes your story. I've said it before; the public can sniff out a phony. Your business will suffer if there is a hint of inauthenticity in your story and no consistency in your cause, *why*, logo, or mission statement.

Chapter 6

FROM LETTERHEAD TO WEBSITE

At the end of Chapter 5, I said that your brand must be consistent. So, I will explain that in this chapter.

You need to stay consistent with your brand in many ways, and they don't all have to do with the same logo on your printed publications and website. Of course, that is part of it, but it's not the whole. So here are the ways John Hall from Forbes tells us to maintain consistency.

1. Your brand image is directly related to your values. You may find that you want to adjust your logo a tiny bit once or so, and you may even get away with a dramatic change. Once. But try to change it too often, and you'll lose the trust you've built with your customers. You don't want them to see you as wishy-washy or a flake.

2. Your logo will be the foundation for everything else within your business: letterhead, business cards, website, emails, and blog posts. All print and electronic publications your business uses must maintain visual consistency. Remember, your logo is the face

of your business, and you want that face to be everywhere. If you want to keep the trust you build with your customers, you must stay consistent with how they see you.

3. As your business grows, you'll find it less stressful to appoint someone whose values and goals align with yours to approve all branding choices. If you have one, this might be your marketing director or even a creative director. It would be unrealistic to think that your business will never grow and that you'll always have the time to make those decisions yourself. However, ensure that whoever you give that task to, will make the decisions you would. The world is full of companies who have had to apologize for mistakes, and you don't want to join that club.

4. Your products and services must always stay to the high standards you set at the start of your business. It's easy for those standards to slip as time passes, but for your brand to stay consistent, that cannot happen. Set up audits or checks and balances to ensure company standards remain where they belong. The public will allow one or two mistakes by a company that requires an apology, but their forgiveness only goes so far. It is much easier to keep your good reputation than to earn it back once a bad reputation has been established.

5. Internal communications must have the same tone as external. Therefore, your company's work culture should be the same as your company's image. For example, you can't be casual and treat your customers like family while you expect formality and a strict dress code from your employees. Whatever image you started projecting to the public must also be within the company. You won't keep employees, and they won't share your values if there is hypocrisy.

You can see how consistency is in more than just the look of your printed and electronic publications. To stay authentic, you must be consistent. Whatever message you're trying to convey to the public should be sent to your employees.

I want to go over a couple more things that must be consistent and then follow up with some steps you can take to keep that consistency.

It's to be expected that one of the most prominent representatives of your brand is your content. Brand consistency is essential. It:
- determines your uniqueness.
- helps you make a name for yourself.
- keeps your company growing.

At some point in your business, you may have more than one writer or content creator. Each one will have their style, their personality. However, within your brand, the
- words
- design
- perspective
- offerings (articles)

… must all relate to how you want your brand expressed. If there is inconsistency in brand content or articles, your brand will lose its authenticity. Customers will be confused, unsure if you know them like they thought you did. So keeping your writers or content creators on the same page is crucial.

Set guidelines for what you want your content to look and sound like. As with everything else, you can review those guidelines periodically and make any necessary updates. But unless something drastic changes within your brand, those guidelines will probably not change much. Your policies should have these elements:
- message: Your content should be clear and easy to understand.
- target audience: It should be clear who your content is addressing.
- voice: The formality or tone of the content should stay the same.
- terminology: Keep track of words that you don't want to be used as well as words you want to be used often.
- writing style: No matter the tone or voice of your content, grammar and punctuation rules should be strictly followed.

There is something within these policies that I would like to address, and that is voice. Some content creators have a formal tone or voice to their writing, while others have a more conversational tone. But it comes down to the voice or tone you want to be used in your content. For example, if your brand is based on treating everyone like family, your tone will be conversational. Therefore, it would be disruptive to your customers if they read an article with a formal, slightly stilted tone.

Voice also follows the idea of consistency and authenticity in your brand. For example, you treat everyone like family, indicating that any content would be conversational. But it would be inconsistent to have a formal tone in your content—something to think about when determining your content policies. Because if you prefer a more formal tone in your content, you will want to align the rest of your brand with that.

If your customers expect one tone based on your purpose or mission statement, but the actual tone is different, they will go to a competitor. It's as simple as that.

So remember that consistency must be in all areas of your brand.
- printed and electronic publications
- content: articles, emails, advertisements, commercials, etc.
- employee environment
- leadership and decision-making

It's not just what your business looks like that is the face of your brand. It is your employees, your content, and the decision-making process. The best way to keep everything consistent and show authenticity is to have company policies and ensure everyone knows and follows them. Honestly, though, if you've got employees who share your vision, it will be easier for them to stay consistent. But you are the brand's core, so it's your lead they will follow, and your lead is in more than just your purpose.

Chapter 7

KNOW THE COMPETITION

You are probably asking yourself why you need to consider the competition while setting up your brand. Well, the first thought is that business is a competition, and don't we all work harder when we know someone out there wants to take first place? Studying the competition is called competitive analysis. In this chapter, I will explain why you should conduct this study and then tell you how to do it. And while I've mentioned before how important each step is, competitive analysis is no different. It is one of the most important things you can do for your business.

Let's start with eight good reasons why you should study the competition:

- First, you don't become complacent: If you stop trying to be better than your competition, you'll stop trying. As I mentioned in the first paragraph of this chapter, we all work harder when we know we have to keep up or pass the competition.
- You create brand awareness: When you work against the competition, you find innovative ways to stand out and become a leader in your field.
- You develop self-awareness: When you pay attention to what the competition is doing, you can see what you are doing that needs to be adjusted.

- You will be encouraged to offer more: When you see what the competition offers, this is your chance to offer your customer more. To prove that you go above and beyond or offer just that little extra because the customer means more to you.
- You can identify and embrace new trends: When you analyze your competition, you may find that they've been doing something the same way for so long that they forget about new technology or new ideas. You will have the opportunity to keep track of the latest trends and offer something a little better or more contemporary than the competition.
- You can create an alliance: It's not always a bad idea to join forces with your competition. Maybe the two of you can offer your customers that little extra if you work together. You don't have to partner with everything, but there may be an event or cause that the two or more of you can work on together. Be a team player, and you may gain access to new technology, tools, or products.
- You can learn: By observing your competition, you will often learn something about the industry you were unaware of. Also, learning from a company that's been doing it for a long time is wise.
- You may develop a niche: You wanted to niche down but weren't sure what you could do. Then, you observe your competition and notice they're not offering something customers have asked you about. Suddenly, you have your niche and your competitive edge.

Here are the three steps on how you should do a competitive analysis:
1. First, identify the competition: If the industry is broad, narrow it down as much as possible so you're not analyzing companies that are too far off the mark for what you're offering. If you've discovered a niche in the market, try to find a competitor close to yours.
2. Analyze the competitors: You're looking at their business strategies while paying close attention to the strengths and weaknesses of the competitor. You must study both because each will aid your brand in its growth and potential.

a. strengths: Paying attention to what the competition does that works will show you what you should be doing.
   b. weaknesses: Studying what your competitors are missing in their business strategy will allow you to use that information to your benefit. If they're missing something, you can do it and gain a competitive edge.
3. Create a grid for competitive strengths: Using the information you've learned from your analysis, create a grid with five areas. You will list critical assets and skills in each area. Also, note if it is a weakness or strength for each competitor. The areas are:
   a. product
   b. distribution
   c. pricing
   d. promotion
   e. advertising

Now that your analysis is complete, what do you do? Well, you do the actual analysis. You've collected your data and sorted it all into the grid, but now you have to analyze it and figure out how to use it to your advantage. Here is what you look for:

- market gaps: Identify the unserved or underserved gaps in the market. Is the competitor charging premium prices for higher quality goods while missing out on the bargain segment of the market? Then they're undeserving the bargain segment, and this is where you can step in. You're willing to offer bargain prices for high-quality goods.
- product development: Figure out their product and how they're improving it or their services. Maybe they're ignoring a key component in their service or product; this is where you can shine.
- market trends: I touched on this earlier in the chapter, but it's important to note that if the competitor is missing out on a specific market trend, you can take advantage of that.

- marketing practices: Besides knowing the competition's products and services, you must study their marketing strategies. For example, how do they market themselves? And how much money do they spend? Another vital piece of information to learn—survey their customers to find out what they think of the competitor. One aspect of customer surveys can be the reviews given on a company's products or services. These reviews provide valuable clues to the competition's customer service and product.

When conducting your research on the competition, check out their prices. If they're charging a lot more for the same product, you can exploit that information in your advertising or change your prices. But also find out about their vendors, which may be the driving force behind their prices. Having this information can inspire creativity in your marketing and branding.

FOLLOW THE COMPETITION'S EXAMPLE

Don't make assumptions when determining what the competition is doing well. For example, you may be wildly off the mark if you assume their success is due to their advertising when it's because of their customer service skills.

You need to pay attention when the competition is number one in the industry. Then do it better. By following the example of a company that's doing it right, you're following a readymade how-to guide. They've done the hard part and learned the right stuff. Now all you have to do is follow their example.

I mentioned that there could be the possibility of an alliance with a competitor. When you discover your competition's strengths, a merger is something to consider, but I don't mean a merger as in selling your business. If you have analyzed your competitor and realized that you could not do better in one area, you may think about approaching them with an idea for the two of you to work together.

You can be assured that they've also analyzed your company, and there may be something you have to offer in exchange for the chance to improve one facet of your business.

LEARN FROM THEIR MISTAKES

By analyzing the competition, you will see what they do that misses the mark or where they are lacking in an area. For example, maybe their advertising on social media sites is low. This means you'll have an edge when you heavily advertise on social media sites. You have to figure that they don't know enough about social media or the internet to promote in those areas successfully. However, why they don't do it isn't as important as the fact that they just don't do it. So you need to make sure it's one thing you do and do well.

Review your practices and adjust what you do to avoid their mistakes. Paying attention to what the competition is doing wrong allows you to use their vulnerabilities to your advantage. Then, you can make sure to do it right without suffering the consequences or pitfalls of making a mistake. This is the time to learn by example rather than by doing.

Chapter 8

COMMUNICATION IS KEY

Branding your business is how you communicate what your product and service stand for. Based on how you communicate, of course, the customer will either embrace or ignore your message. Therefore, I've got some advice from 12 communications experts on the Forbes Communication Council about how to communicate effectively to the customer. Let's see what they have to say:

- Do some experiential marketing: What a great effective way to create unique and memorable moments with customers. It's a way to connect through experiences such as pop-up stores, mobile events, or even fancy parties. There is no limit to this marketing strategy, but remember that it must make sense to the customer. Whatever experience you choose must align with your cause. So make sure the brand is consistent with the experience.
- Show your brand in real-time: Sometimes, customers wonder when they would use a product or service. So show them. Use videos or live streaming in offices or stores that show real people using your product or service. This will give an instant answer to that question.
- It's all about the swag: Branded swag speaks volumes, and most people will not turn down free stuff. So have your staff decked out

in branded clothing that shows off your brand colors and logo. Have them use branded mugs, water bottles, pens, etc. Better yet, give away branded swag to customers—what a way to grab the customer's attention.
- Self-Service: When customers can choose how and when they take advantage of offers, you will have a greater opportunity to interact on their terms. You can also build customer profiles while learning their preferences by utilizing self-service. You'll know when to be proactive, engaging with them when they're ready to hear what you say.
- Guidelines must be clear and cover it all: For your marketing team to create everything you need to set your brand, make sure your policies are clear. But also ensure you've covered everything from the logo and font to the emotions you want to be elicited from customers. Finally, give your marketing team all the tools they'll need to set your brand's consistency.
- Step outside the box: Your brand is unique, so don't think you must follow all the rules when designing your logo, store sign, etc. For example, your store name is long? Why does the font have to be sized to fit the building? Let it dangle off at the end or wrap around a corner. Color outside the picture! Remember, you're trying to catch your customer's eyes.
- Consistent online and in-store experiences: Consistency is the key, and whatever experience your customers have in your store must carry over to your website. Your customers must recognize all facets of the brand, whether shopping online or browsing your store shelves.
- Show off your company culture: Your customers expect authenticity, so show them what you're doing. Set up a display, both in-store and online, that showcases an event you hosted for the cause you have. Put together a slideshow of pictures on your website and a monitor in the store. Let customers see images from

a charitable event in which you participated. Remember, you told your target audience you shared their passion-now show them the proof.
- Your in-store space should be a content campaign: It's the digital age, and your shoppers would love to have an interactive experience while in your store. So keep your space alive with digital displays of brand and influencer content. Then choose brand hashtags so your shoppers can join the conversation through social media platforms. This makes your customers feel like they are family and a part of your brand.
- Grassroots: This is where you keep yourself at the front of your business. Meet with your employees for lunch while all of you are wearing your branded clothing. Wear your branded clothing when picking up your coffee before or after work, and maybe even hand out a few pieces of branded swag while at the coffee shop.
- Stay consistent: I know that consistency is crammed down your throat in this book, but it is the ultimate key to all of this. Everything you do, even in-store, must be brand consistent—colors, logo, customer interaction, right down to the feel or vibe of the store. Outside the building, your bathrooms—don't miss a spot. When customers enter your store, they should feel immersed in your brand. They've entered your brand's world, and you want to embrace them with that world.
- Show your story: When setting your brand, you're like a writer being told, "Show, don't tell." But it's on point. You need to show the story behind your brand, the product you put on the shelves, or the service you offer. For example, a collage of your pictures that depict you using the product in some aspect of your story. For instance, you carry a book from the store while feeding the hungry. Maybe you and a group of friends read together in the store. Or you are reading to a group of kids. Whatever your cause, it includes your product or service, so show customers that

story. They want to be inspired to buy your product or use your service—inspire them!

FIND YOUR VOICE

Katie Wertsch tells us about finding our brand voice in her article "*How to Find Your Brand Voice.*" In fact, according to Wertsch, your brand voice goes back to the beginning of setting your brand. She mentions the original questions you asked yourself when you first decided to start a business.

- What do you want to accomplish?
- What is the problem you're trying to solve?
- How do you want to solve the problem?
- Who needs your help?

But then she tosses out a new question that has to do with voice.

- How do you want your customers to see you and your business?

We haven't addressed this question yet, but it's the one you need to answer to find your voice. Because by figuring that out and getting it right, your customers will be able to see and understand your brand when they find you.

First, I like what Wertsch says about branding, and I think you need to hear it.

"Branding is the act of communicating the heart and soul of your business to your customers."

That is beautiful, and it sums up the first seven chapters of this book in one statement. Pretty powerful.

But to keep moving forward, you probably already know your voice. You just need to figure out how to communicate that voice to the public and your customers. Here are the steps Wertsch gives us to work out the details of your brand voice:

- reflect: This first step is when you sit down and reflect on who you are and your business's goal. First, list your core values: what

personality traits and rules you believe are crucial to successfully operating your business. Be thorough with your list; missing even one key point could skew your results. Then, going back to the first couple of chapters in this book, you need to write notes on your:
- purpose (why)
- vision (what)
- mission (why)

- who: Write out buyer personas for your target audience. A buyer persona is a hypothetical character sheet of the person you believe will want to use your service or buy your product. To complete this step, you will need to consider:
  - demographics
  - location
  - likes and dislikes
  - goals
  - roadblocks to your buyer's goals
  - objections your buyer may have to your product or service

Putting together these buyer personas takes a few steps. First, you can get some information from past customers. You can send out surveys to get all the information, including demographics and location. If you have a sales team, they will be a gold mine of information since they are in touch with the public. Finally, review sales information for specifics like trends and average price points. Another piece of information that is valuable to gather is how people heard about your business. This will give you insight into marketing strategies.

- differential advantage: You've figured out your buyer persona, but now you have to figure out what sets you apart from your competitors. Go further than product or excellent customer service. What about your you-core values, ideals, etc.-that sets you above the rest? What is so unique about you that it will draw in your customers?

- brainstorm the brand: The tough branding questions should be a team effort. So get your team together for this last step in finding your brand voice. While brainstorming, note how your team communicates; what tone, vocabulary, and voice do they use? Knowing what your team contributes will help you figure out your brand voice. But this brainstorming session should answer these questions:
    - How do we want customers to feel when they interact with the brand?
    - What adjectives describe the brand?
    - How is the brand voice different from the competitor's brand voice?
    - What other brand voices do we love?
    - How do we want to talk about ourselves?
    - Who do we not want to be?

Remember, your brand voice is the verbal expression of your business. You set the visual expression with your logo, colors, signage, etc. Now you need to express those emotions verbally. This brand voice will be everything verbal, from advertisements to website information to emails.

A strong brand identity will help you stand out from the competitors but, more importantly, will help you connect with the right people.

Chapter 9

THE TOOLS FOR BUILDING A BRAND

You need resources and tools to help you stay organized when building your brand. There is much more to building a brand besides identity and voice. Once you've established the brand, you must keep it moving forward. You can't sit back and let it run itself because it won't. Your brand must grow and expand, and you must perform reviews regularly.

This chapter will list the tools and resources you'll need to keep your brand running smoothly and expanding as it should. Remember, in chapter seven, you learned that you must always be aware of your competition to experience continued success. Some of the tools and resources mentioned here will help you track your progress. You need to be vigilant and never let your guard down. It's always going to be a race to stay ahead of the competition, and by utilizing the tools and resources available to you, staying in the top spot will be within your grasp.

You will probably choose to hire a team to handle a lot of the behind-the-scenes stuff; the operations. But you will need these tools to make their job easier and ensure the business runs smoothly. And if you choose to do much of it yourself, you'll find that having these tools at hand makes your life easier.

RESOURCES

Your brand will require content for your website, and if you don't have your website done by professionals, you will need the following content creation resources.
- Unsplash
- Rawpixel
- Pexels
- MixKit
- Burst
- By People
- Envato Elements

Communities

Within the resources listed above, you need to be aware of the communities you can use for information about your target audience. These communities offer insight into what your target audience is looking for, along with their dislikes. You want to know everything about your target audience, and using the following communities will give you pertinent data about your customers. Don't assume. Know. And get it straight from the customers.
- Quora
- Social Media
- Groups and Forums

TOOLS AND SERVICES

- Management tools: This tool will let you keep track of your ideas. Organization is the key to following your well-laid plans, and

note-taking is the first step. You may not always be in a position to put your ideas into practice, but it is entirely possible that you will forget something if you don't make a note of it. This tool can be a digital note-taking program, or you can take notes by hand, whichever is your preference. Some do both. Here is a short list of digital note-taking tools that you can use if you prefer to keep notes on your phone or computer:
  - Evernote
  - Google Keep
  - One Note
  - Notion
- Project Management tools: These tools will help you keep track of your projects and workflow—an excellent way to stay organized and keep you productive.
  - Zenkit
  - Trello
  - Slack
  - Asana
- Document Management tools: Every business needs tools to assist in looking professional with their documents, and this tool is perfect for that task. This tool you will use specifically in your workplace, since it consists of things like spreadsheets. You must show organization and professionalism when communicating with vendors or government officials, regardless of your brand identity or voice.
  - Microsoft Office
  - Google Docs
  - Open Office
- Storage tools: Almost everyone is going paperless, and your business will probably be no exception. Rather than multiple filing cabinets jammed full of old paperwork and files, you must save for a specified time; you will need storage devices to hold all

that stuff digitally. Plus, you will want to share specific files with employees or possible government offices.
- Google Drive
- One Drive
- Dropbox

Website Tools

Even if you think you won't need a website, you will eventually discover that you do. Having the proper tools will make it much easier for your daily work. Whoever you hire for this position will appreciate the tools, as well.

- Domain Management tools: If you choose to set up your website rather than having the expense of hiring it out, you will need one to help you find your domain and the right website generator for you.
  - Namecheap
  - Bluehost
  - GoDaddy

Website Building tools: Again, if you're building your website yourself or you've hired someone to come in and take care of that for you, you'll need the tool to put it together. Your website should be a special place representing your brand identity and voice. Therefore, you can't just toss it together, so you should put time and effort into it. I recommend you find someone knowledgeable about this, since you also want it to look professional. Of course, you can find a professional service to build and maintain your website, but if you can hire an in-house person for that job, you'll have someone strictly devoted to your website. They will also be someone who understands your brand voice and identity. The first three on the list are plugins through WordPress, but the last two are excellent options if you don't like WordPress.
- Elementor
- Yoast

- Hummingbird
- Wix
- Square Space
- Social Management tools: You will find that advertising on social media platforms is lucrative and time-consuming. However, it is also a vital marketing tool. To track and manage your social media marketing, you will need one of the following tools to keep you organized in the overwhelming world of social media. Social media marketer is another position you may need to fill within your brand, especially if it's not something you want to tackle. For example, the position could be a communications specialist, so they would do more than just social media.
  - Later
  - Buffer
  - Sprout Social
  - Facebook Creator Studio

Editing Tools

There will always come a time in any business when you need a tool to help you edit the flyer you're creating or the email you're sending. The following tools will give you that extra nudge you need to send out the most professional-looking content. Whether your company is informal or formal, grammar and punctuation are vital to your brand identity, as are the images you present to your customers.

- Canva
- Visme
- Adobe
- Grammarly

Marketing Tools

Email is still one of the main ways to market your brand, and specific tools will help you with that portion of marketing.

- Sendinblue
- ConvertKit
- Mailchimp
- Constant Contact

Because there are other ways to market your brand, multiple tools can help you in those areas.

- Headline Analyzer
- Keywords Everywhere
- Moz SEO Tools

Analytics Tools

These tools will go along with the website tools. Part of your strategy is ensuring that customers find you on the website. These tools will tell you how your brand does in search engines. If something lacking within your marketing techniques keeps you from being one of the first brands a customer sees when they do a Google search, you need to be aware of it to make necessary adjustments.

- Google Search Console
- Google Trends
- Answer The Public
- Similar Web
- Google Analytics
- SumAll

So from taking notes to analyzing your website, there are tools and resources to help you build every corner of your brand. Use as many of them as you can, and by all means, try them all out. Unless you are already familiar with them, you won't know which ones suit you until you try them.

But remember to use what you have at your fingertips, as well. Build a team. Yes, this is your brand; you've put in the blood, sweat, and tears.

Your values are out there for all to see and criticize. But don't forget that you can be stronger when you build a team within this brand.

If managing a website intimidates you, find someone to do it for you. Find someone who shares your values and vision and would love to put your brand identity online for you. Use your strengths, then find people to fill in the blanks where your weaknesses are. Once you've established your team, remember to keep it running as a team. Your brand and your customers will appreciate it. And so will you, because after keeping that brand going for a few years, you will be ready to move on to the next section of this book.

Part Two
Selling Your Business

Chapter 1

FIGURING OUT YOUR EXIT STYLE

You built your brand, and it's been successful. But years of being front and center in that brand, trying to stay ahead of the competition while keeping your growing target audience content has started to take its toll. Or maybe your brand has grown too much, and you miss the small business feel. Perhaps you're ready to sell and start another brand. No matter the circumstances, you're prepared to put your exit strategy into motion.

And you want to put the same consideration into selling the brand that you did when you built it. Therefore, you will want to begin planning your exit strategy in advance. Even if it takes years or decades to put that plan into motion, there are benefits to having one ready:

- Your brand will follow a chosen path: You've spent so much time determining your company's vision, but there is another goal you must keep in your sights. No matter how you choose to leave the company, there will come an end to your time with it. Knowing how you'll take that step will ensure the consistency that you have

been laser-focused on. Surprises should be the last thing you want, especially when you've spent so much time and effort building your brand.
- You will stay committed to finances: Yes, I've stressed how making money is simply a product of your business and should not be the main component of your decisions. And it still isn't. However, if you know that your exit strategy will consist of selling the company or going public, you have to keep its monetary value up. Your company should have more than an emotional value; it should also hold economic value.
- Your company will appeal to buyers: Buyers will be more interested in your company if they know that your commitment extends to preparing a viable exit strategy and building a brand. In addition, your pledge to the brand's vision and goals will ensure interest in your company when it comes time to make your exit.
- Looking for that smooth transition: When you've prepared everything in advance, you can take your exit without disrupting your brand more than is necessary. Remember, you poured your heart and soul into the company. Therefore, don't let even a thread of negative energy come up when you leave.
- Prevent unwanted consequences: Putting together your exit strategy now can eliminate any potential consequences that could take place after a surprise, unexpected exit. Because you will meticulously lay out each step, you will successfully remove the possibility of something like bankruptcy. You have only ever wanted to see this brand succeed.

Before you decide on your business exit strategy, though, you need to ask yourself three questions:
- First, how long do you want to stay with the business?
- Second, what is your financial target?
- Third, who will you need to pay off before you leave?

Once you've answered these questions, there are six steps you need to take. I will go over each of them in the following chapters, but here is a short list:
- prepare finances
- consider options
- discuss with investors
- choose leadership
- tell employees
- inform customers

You will prepare an exit strategy and have the plans ready once your business is off the ground, and you may wait a beat before you start getting your plan together. But the above-listed steps are the ones you will take once you're ready to put the plan into motion.

UNDERSTAND THE OPTIONS

There are more options than you would realize when following an exit strategy. All of them take careful planning and preparation because even one that sounds like it would be the easiest requires thought. Ultimately, your decision is going to come from what your goal is.
- Are you looking for a sound retirement plan?
- Do you want to leave a legacy?
- Do you want your business to end with your exit?

There are a lot of things to take into consideration, but you're up to the challenge. You had a vision when you started your business, and it's safe to say that you will also have an idea of what the end looks like.

Selling

Ideally, you can sell to a trusted buyer—one who shares your passion and is willing to continue your legacy. However, there are drawbacks to this idea that you need to keep in mind. For instance:

- Because you know the buyer, you may be tempted to sell at a price lower than the company's value.
- If you sell to a family member, this can cause tensions down the road between you and the family member, which can have repercussions on the business.

However, if you sell to someone you don't know, you can still find someone who shares your vision and will continue your legacy. Moreover, whether the buyer is someone you know or a stranger, if they don't have the funds to pay the total price (and who does), they will pay for it over time. This brings about some significant advantages:

- The buyer does not have an enormous upfront cost and can run the business without that hanging over their head, and you will have a guaranteed income each month.
- You can remain with the company as a mentor while the seller acclimates to the brand and its vision.
- The transition will be smooth because the buyer has a stake in the business, and the employees and customers can ease into your exit.

Now, if you sell to a large corporation, you must consider a few things. For example, will they be willing to continue the company's vision, or will that change? On the other hand, you'll make more money because a large business will have the funds to 1) pay more and 2) pay you the total asking amount. But, again, you'll have to worry that the climate of your brand will change. Because it's a large business buying out a smaller company, will there be layoffs? Your employees are like family, and there's a strong chance that some of them will lose their job. In addition, customers might be put off by a more prominent company or corporation running the brand, and some of your target customers might move over to the competitor.

So the bottom line is that if you choose to sell, you also have to decide whether you sell to an individual or another company.

Mergers & Acquisitions

Mergers and acquisitions can be lucrative, and your exit strategy may be just what you're looking for. Besides, this exit style can be beneficial to the brand and employees. So keep that in mind while you look over these benefits:

- increased size equals more efficiency: This is called Economies of Scale, which comes about when merging two companies. It's when a more prominent company acquires a smaller one that offers better service and products to customers; although a larger company may have more, you may have something they don't. Once they acquire your business, they gain that something without the cost and time put into achieving it, but it makes their business better. It may be one small thing, but it may be the one small thing they need to realize the ultimate success in their company.
- economies of scope: This benefit is all about efficiency. Your company might have a service or product that the larger one does not offer for whatever reason. So it might make sense to merge the companies, giving them that something you do that enhances what they have.
- talent: You may have an employee with unparalleled skill, and the larger company knows this. They also know the only way to access this talent is to have it for themselves, but your employee refuses to leave. So what are they to do but acquire your company for themselves, giving them access to the skill set they're looking for?
- resources: Again, your small company may have access to a resource that the larger company needs. How else to get it but with your company? Not only will they gain valuable employees who are the best at what they do, but they'll also have access to that resource. It doesn't always have to do with the production

- of a product; it could be a resource sold only to your company because of good contract negotiations.
- spreading the risk: When a larger company buys your smaller brand, they want to spread the risk. In other words, if one of their sources of revenue dries up or has been struggling, they won't lose money because they'll have your source of income to fall back on.
- nobody wants to start from scratch: If a larger company has wanted to branch off in another direction or add to what they already do, one of their hesitations might be start-up costs. It may be something in which they'll have to have a new facility or learn how to do something different, or even add another product. But, on the other hand, your company has already done the hard work, and the facilities are ready to go. So no start-up fee for the big company, but they reap the rewards.
- new markets: This is another benefit of the time, effort, and money you've put into the brand. The more prominent companies may realize the potential if you've got the market cornered on a specific product or service. However, they're not ready to put that same effort into it, but acquiring your business will give them what they want. You will see this more often in companies who wish to become international, a problematic aspect of any market. So if your company has already gone through the red tape and the hassle, well, you see the point.
- your brand value: Your company's value is one thing to consider when deciding to use mergers and acquisitions as your exit strategy. Unless you have something that the competitors are beating down your door for, mergers generally occur when a smaller company is in financial distress. The more prominent companies don't want to throw money away, so they will look for a bargain. It's a win-win situation because the smaller company stays in business while the larger one has gained valuable employees, products, and resources.

- continuing your vision: Your company may always be a small business privately owned by you and your family. Therefore, the risk is significant that the company will dissolve upon your death or your happy retirement, where you hand the business over to your kids. Merging with a larger company before retirement will ensure that your legacy and vision continue.
- Overall, using mergers and acquisitions as your exit strategy is tricky and requires research and a thorough understanding of the process. In addition, you may want to think about the paperwork and the extra hassle that may come with this style.

IPO (Initial Public Offering)

An IPO is when a company goes from private to public. In other words, your company will have shareholders and a place in the stock market. Many people view this as a desirable outcome, while others avoid it as long as possible. This is another exit strategy that will require an excessive amount of paperwork and research. Every step to the smallest must be laid out in advance because things can get tricky in this area. Fast.

Your brand may have a few investors as a private company, but they will probably consist of family and friends. Venture capitalists may have chipped in with an investment, as well. But going public is a big step because it proves that your company has reached a valuation of about $1 billion, or you can prove that the company is mature enough to handle what comes with going public. As a publicly traded company, your brand will have the additional burden of responsibility toward the shareholders, which can be an added stress to succeed. As a public company, you're telling shareholders that your company can be successful enough to offer them the benefits they're looking for.

An IPO is a good way for you, the founder or biggest private investor in your brand, to make money off your investment. You've been making money, or you wouldn't be eligible for an IPO. However, it's time to 1) sell shares for a considerable profit, 2) keep some and watch profits grow, or 3) leave the investment entirely.

There is a lot of information packed into the IPO exit strategy route, but I will let you do your research on the details. First, however, I want to break it down and give you some ideas of what comes with using an IPO exit route. They are:

- sell your stake in the company: As the founder, you are the primary investor in your brand, so after an IPO, you should have many shares. If you choose to use this exit style, you will have the opportunity to sell those shares.
- lock-in period: After an IPO, there is a lock-in period of approximately 3 to 24 months before you can sell your shares. Make sure you know what this time is since you'll want to do it right to maximize your profits.
- sell in pieces: You may sell your shares in chunks rather than all at once. This is up to you, of course. But it depends on two things:
  - Do you want to keep a piece of the company and some shares?
  - Do you want to separate from the brand entirely?

Here are some terms for you to investigate while doing your research for this particular exit route:

- Primary Market
- Secondary Market
- Float
- Market Price and Market Valuation*
- Issue Price
- Flipping
- Lock-in Period

The market price or valuation is a term I will be covering in one of the following chapters of this book. You will need to have a market valuation done, whether selling the brand or doing an IPO.

There are a couple of options when you decide to sell your private equity shares in the company after the lock-in period. For starters, you can sell privately, which can be challenging. Selling to a private investor does not get you the best return on those shares; the price may be a little low. This is because there is no accurate way to know how much value the public market has yet placed on the company and the private investors want to make money, so they're going to try to buy for a lower price while hoping to sell later for a higher price.

Selling publicly after the lock-in period may be more manageable. But you would be wise to sell in parts because a large batch of shares being sold at once will trigger a panic in the market, which will cause share prices to fall. However, selling your shares publicly is better because there's a better chance of finding a buyer, and their value will be considerably higher than your original investment.

I am not covering all facets of an IPO because this topic is lengthy and detailed. Skimming the surface will only confuse you further. It's best to use professional assistance while navigating this exit strategy, especially when considering an IPO. But this book will give you some things to think about while you make your decisions.

So here are the key points you need to remember about using an IPO as your exit strategy:

- It can be an effective exit route.
- You can sell your private equity shares to the public after the lock-in period.
- Publicly selling your private equity shares will bring you a more significant reward, since the value will be much higher than your initial investment.
- You can hold onto some of those private equity shares, giving you a small stake in the company.
- Remember to sell your shares in batches so there's no dramatic drop in stock prices.

Liquidation or Closing

Many people think that liquidating or closing your business is the most straightforward exit strategy that doesn't require much paperwork or effort. However, that is incorrect. No matter what exit route you choose, you must make many decisions and paperwork must be filed. You can't just walk away from a business and let it dissolve on its own. Not easily, anyway, and there will be repercussions if you go that route. So here are some tips and things to think about if you are thinking about liquidating your brand.

There are a couple of ways to close your business. One is called "lifestyle business," which means closing your business over time. You keep the business open, pay yourself until the money is gone, and close it up. However, this has more drawbacks than you'd realize. One is that you will upset any investors you may have, and you will upset employees.

The business growth is stunted by doing this, and quite honestly, you're just abandoning that vision you had when you set your purpose and mission statement. At the point of closing the business, that might not matter to you. However, it can hurt your business because if you change your mind midstream and decide to sell, the valuation of your business drops considerably. By closing your business this way, you have cut off the ability for the brand to grow, so there's no more value to it.

Your other option is to close the business and sell the assets. This creates hardship, also, and there is no monetary value in this for you. Nothing to set aside for retirement because you must pay your creditors and employees' last checks before you pay yourself. The only money you will make is from selling your assets, and if the closing is done hurriedly, you will probably not get the highest prices for those assets.

Of course, the amount you make from selling the assets will also depend on your real estate. Do you own the building you operate out of or rent it? You will have even less time to sell and get out if you rent. If you own, you can probably take a little longer to get more money from what you sell, but then you have to figure out the real estate market. When it's time to close up shop, is it a buyer or seller market? How much will you have after selling the building and other assets and paying creditors? That's a lot of number crunching.

Of course, there's still paperwork and further small details to take care of. Before you've closed the business and sold everything and then paid off creditors, you have paperwork and other details to consider before you're out. They are:
- file dissolution paperwork
- cancel unnecessary business expenses
    - registrations
    - licenses
    - business name
- close employee payments, ensuring that you comply with federal and state labor laws
- file final taxes
    - keep the records for the legally advised length of time
        - usually, three to seven years

There is a lot to consider when determining your exit strategy. Naturally, things change as time goes by, and after a few years, you may change your mind about the style you choose. However, if you've done thorough research, it should be easy to change it once you've made a new decision.

Chapter 2

GETTING YOUR DUCKS IN A ROW

I ended the last chapter talking about the paperwork that must be taken care of when you close your business, and I'd like to begin this chapter with a little of the same. There will always be paperwork that needs to be completed and filed, federal and state laws to follow, and labor laws to pay attention to. In addition, some steps must be taken within the brand when making your exit, no matter the style you've chosen. I will try to break it down as much as possible in this chapter.

LEGAL

Everything is essential when you've made your exit style choice, so the order in which I am offering the information in this chapter is not in any specific order for a reason. You simply need to complete each one.

However, after saying that, I would say that the legal documents are probably at the top of the list. You need to know about these in advance. Put together an exit advisory team a little before the time comes for you to begin your exit strategy.

Most importantly, have a lawyer specializing in business exits because you do not want any loopholes or complications if the wrong paperwork is filed or filed incorrectly. In addition, if you perform the research in advance, you will save time with the many questions you will have when the exit strategy takes place. Naturally, you'll also need someone to draft the documents; the lawyer will be your go-to person for that task.

Letters of Intent

A letter of intent, or LOI, is a written document that spells out the offer for your business. It details the price, structure, and terms the potential buyer proposes.

The LOI allows you to identify critical components and begin negotiations. But, of course, this document also allows you to decide if the offer is acceptable or if the buyer should look elsewhere.

You will choose an LOI that is the best fit financially and personally. For instance, if the buyer is proposing deferred payments, you will need to have their creditworthiness checked before agreeing to anything.

Sometimes a seller will want to continue working for the business, which may not be your desire. However, if it is a step you choose, you will need to ensure the details, such as length of time and salary rate, are also worked out. In other words, every little piece of the sale, from minor to the big stuff, needs to be spelled out and then finessed before you accept anything.

Purchase and Sale Agreement

The Purchase and Sale Agreement document, or P & S Agreement, is sometimes called the Definitive Purchase Agreement. This one is the heart of the papers in your exit strategy. Everything, down to the smallest detail, will be included in this one. It is very long and very detailed. Therefore, this is not a document that just anyone can complete. Your legal counsel will write this one. The attorney you've lined up to be on your Exit Strategy Advisory Team will give advice and expertise while the document is being prepared.

You will need to talk to your tax advisor about this document, as well, since it will be one of two agreements.

- Stock Purchase Agreement
- Asset Purchase Agreement

The tax implications are very different, and your accountant must adequately address that distinction within your exit strategy and the end taxes.

Naturally, all the minor and major details and clauses you could think of while working on your LOI will be in this agreement. Because if it isn't in this document, then it's not a thing in the sale of your brand. Therefore, no matter how tedious, you'll need to go over every detail of the P & S Agreement before it's signed.

Non-Compete Agreements

Buyers of any business must be concerned with the existing owner; in this case, you, becoming their biggest competitor. As the brand's founder, you are most familiar with and adept at the business. The last thing your successor wants is to have competition from you if you decide to leave and start another similar company. Even if your new company niches down even more, competition from you can put them out of business.

So a non-compete agreement is just what it sounds like. You will sign a formal agreement agreeing not to work in the field or start a new business. So you cannot sell your company and work for your biggest competitor. The length of time this agreement is binding will be worked out and noted in the document. Generally, it is six months to a year, but the timing is up to your successor. Non-compete agreements are not usually longer than that since it's considered unreasonable to make someone wait too long to start a new job or possibly work elsewhere. Besides, as I've mentioned before, competition is a good thing in business.

A non-compete clause will probably be a given in your exit strategy, so you should not be surprised. It has pros and cons, but remember, it won't be forever. State laws will determine the duration since each state has requirements for this restriction. However, it is almost certain that it will be required.

The bottom line is that a non-compete agreement will ensure your successor that you will not be handing out trade secrets while they're adjusting to the business. As a result, they have some time to get used to the secrets of your brand, and they have time to implement some innovative ideas before others hear about them.

Earn-Out Agreements

The Earn-Out Agreement will be one of the most carefully worded documents in your exit strategy. This is a tricky part of the exit, and the wording must be precise to protect you and the buyer. The Earn-Out document stipulates how the seller will make payments to you after closing. The business's success determines the payments after you've left. This gets tricky because it is difficult to accurately depict what that will look like.

Naturally, like most sellers, you prefer receiving more money when the sale closes rather than relying on uncertain funds afterward. However, the Earn-Out Agreement is protection for the buyer. Realistically, you know you will be losing control of the business and its progress once you're gone, and it's going to be challenging to rely on funds that will fluctuate due to that lack of control.

To keep the process fair, you must ensure a specific formula and an objective way to determine the business's performance. The level of uncertainty is for you and the buyer, though, making the particular wording of this document of utmost importance.

Seller Financing Agreements

If you sell your business and have accepted deferred payments, you will need a Seller Financing Agreement in your exit plan. This document is generally used when a family member takes over the business. With this agreement, you will not receive money at the closing, but instead, you'll take a note that guarantees you future payments. Naturally, there is usually an interest rate included.

Generally, you will want to find someone with plenty of money to purchase the business, especially if you're taking deferred payments. Your goal is to make money on the sale of your brand.

All these documents aid both you and the buyer. The wording and the details will help you negotiate future interactions with the seller and avoid possible lawsuits because you did not address something during the exit strategy. Paying attention to specifics and addressing everything, no matter how minor it feels, will give you and your buyer peace of mind.

FINANCIAL

The financial paperwork is vital to preparing your exit strategy. Understanding your finances will let you know when it's time to begin your exit from the business. The first thing you need to do is prepare financial statements. These are the foundation of financial reporting because they tell the complete story of your business and its finances. Financial statements will aid you in keeping track and analyzing the business' profit performance. Financial statements must be prepared regularly throughout your time with the business. When you begin your exit strategy, you will need to know your company's finances, and you must keep them up-to-date.

Financial statements will:
- show you where your business is, financially.
  - help you determine accomplishments.

- - help you recognize what you need to do before you leave the company.
  - show you where you are when it comes to your financial target.
  - provide information to gauge your company's value and how much you should sell for.
  - detect trends in earnings and expenditures.
  - provide insight into your business strategies and how you make financial decisions.

Financial statements contain four basic reports:
- income statement
- balance sheet
- statement of cash flows
- statement of retained earnings

Your business should provide an Annual Report to your shareholders (if any), investors, and employees. Anyone with a vested interest in your company.

This report includes:
- the company's ability to pay its debts.
- the previous year's profits and losses.
- business growth.
- retained earnings that helped the company expand.
- operational expenses portion of revenue.

There are some vital sections to this Annual Report:
- company information
- operating and financial features
- CEO's letter to shareholders (if applicable)
- Management's Discussion and Analysis (MD & A)
- financial statements
- notes to financial statements
- auditor's report
- summary of financial data
- accounting policies

These reports are all detailed, and there are a lot. It can seem daunting when you go over the lists above; however, this area of your company is one that you will most likely hire a professional to take care of. No matter who prepares your financial reports and takes care of the money side of your business, you must know everything on those reports. You must at least pay attention to what and how your company is doing financially.

MARKETING

A marketing strategy is another essential piece to your exit strategy puzzle that you probably have not thought of. But the marketing strategy will be your blueprint, the map you will follow with each step of the way clearly identified and planned.

You're probably thinking about how strange it would be to boost your marketing when you plan on leaving the company. However, it makes sense when you think about it. As mentioned in this chapter, your exit strategy goal is to make a profit. What better way to do that than to increase sales? And what is your best plan for upping sales? Marketing, of course.

A surge in new customers and a renewed interest in your brand will be what you need to raise your company's value, making it appealing to potential buyers. However, your team's marketing plan will also need to ensure that your company is up-to-date in your field. And doing all the work to update your company will only add to the value, giving you more for your retirement. The result makes it a win-win for you.

But don't just start randomly updating. Instead, conduct an audit of your processes and content to determine what needs to be updated.

Here are the five marketing strategies that Forbes details:
- Account-Based Marketing Strategy: Simply put, you will identify and pursue the leads that offer the highest value. Once you've determined who those customers are, you will create messages and content to target them.

- Sales and Marketing Alignment: Your sales and marketing teams will work closely for this portion. Marketers appeal to your target audience while sales close the deal and foster relationships with the customers.
- Omni-Channel Marketing: Messaging and branding unite! This strategy will get your company looking relevant to potential customers. The omni-channel approach shows customers what they need but doesn't overwhelm them or scare them away. It's subtle. For instance, a customer spends some time watching a video on your website but does not order. Instead, an email is generated with an invitation to speak to a sales rep for more information. To fully implement this strategy, you should expand your presence to more social media platforms.
- Content Strategy and Development: Content marketing will never go out of style, but you will if you don't keep up with the almost continuous changes. Your customers want transparency, so give it to them. Create blog posts that highlight customer stories or put together some case studies. Maybe it's time to write some e-books about your brand, sharing helpful information. Top of the list is video content. You know what I say: "Lights, camera, action!"

Increasing your company's value is never a waste of time; marketing will give your business the necessary tune-up. Besides, you spent a lot of time and effort building the brand, so you should leave it better than you started it. It's your legacy, after all.

WITHIN THE BRAND

Some critical people within the business need to know your plans. For example, not only do you want to exit the company on top, but you also want to leave behind some goodwill. You've made promises. Everyone within your company has put their faith, and some of their money, in your brand. So keep that in mind while figuring out your exit strategy and follow the next few steps.

Talk to Your Investors

These people believed in your vision and willingly gave you their money. You must approach them with your exit plan, either as soon as you decide you need one or before they've entrusted their money to you. Many investors won't invest until they know what your exit strategy is. They want to ensure they'll be repaid when you take the necessary steps to leave the company.

Nobody wants to be considered your lending tree, so have the following information for investors when you discuss your exit strategy.
- Your financial target.
- Their role in the exit.
- The business milestones.

Most importantly, show them your financial statements and let them know your plans for how they will get back their money. Or if you've promised them returns, let them know how you've prepared for that.

Talk to Employees

Once your plans are in place, you must tell your employees, business partners, and suppliers. Some have probably been with you since the beginning, or at least a while. Naturally, there will be questions, and you want to answer them truthfully. Be upfront with them about your and the new owner's expectations, and try to answer as many questions as possible. It might feel overwhelming, but remember that it will also be overwhelming for these people. Any time there's a transition in a business, employees are left with the fear they may lose their job. You may be able to reassure them about this. If you can't, then be as upfront as possible.

Tell Customers

Your customers, especially the ones who have shown strong brand loyalty, should know about the exit once the plans are in motion. You may be able to introduce the new owner. Plan some sort of event, if possible. If your exit strategy involves closing the business, you will want to have another company to direct your customers to. This kindness can be beneficial to you as well as the customer.

Chapter 3

DETERMINING THE SALE PRICE

The rule of thumb is that a business sells between two and four times the Seller's Discretionary Earnings (SDE) range. However, most companies sell between two and three times this SDE. So, for example, if your company's annual cash flow is $300,000, then you will potentially sell for between $600,000 and $900,000. But first, figure out your company's worth or market value.

Your price should be competitive yet reasonable. If you price too low, buyers may be scared away, thinking there's something sketchy going on. Moreover, they will question the validity of the sale. However, if your price is too high, you'll be considered unreasonable, and nobody will make an offer.

Therefore, you need a business valuation, which is how a company's history, brand, products, and markets are translated into dollars and cents. Although both an art and a science, the objective of each valuation can determine the results. For example, if you decide to take your company public, you need a higher valuation to justify that process. But if you're looking at the value for tax purposes, you'll want a lower number.

Think about this. All business valuations are:
- estimates of economic value.
- influenced by who does it and why.
- not the same as pricing.

Valuations are intrinsic; they are based on the actual performance of your business. But pricing comes from supply and demand while considering market influences such as other investors, news, rumors, and the overall direction of prices. And remember, there are no shortcuts to the complex process of a business valuation. However, it is only an estimate but a valuable one.

GETTING A PROFESSIONAL VALUATION

Remember that there's a professional service for just about everything, and determining your company's value is one of those services. So, I would recommend you have the valuation done by a professional.

Of course, you can try it yourself. But there are a few things to keep in mind while trying to work it all out, and you should only do it yourself if you just want to get a basic understanding of your company's value.

And there are several reasons why it would be easier to hire someone to do it for you.

Generally, business valuations are performed by professionals. These professionals are CPAs Accredited in Business Valuation (ABV). They've passed the specialized exam and have met The American Institute of Certified Public Accountants' minimum standards, earning this specialized certification.

Any time you try to get funded by a lender, investment banker, or venture capitalist, you will be required to have an ABV-certified professional do your business valuation. Think of it like this: You wouldn't have your home appraised by a neighbor when you decide to sell and move; you would use a professional.

HOW TO VALUE THE COMPANY

The condition of your business and the valuation purpose will determine the method. For example, if your business is healthy and generating a profit, your ABV-certified professional will probably use the first method listed here:

- Discounted cash flow: This method calculates five years of your present earnings that have been adjusted for growth plus terminal value, which is the unknown future earnings beyond five years.
- Net Asset, or Book, Value: This method only measures the tangible assets and is usually used for a lower valuation range. The calculation is the fair market value of assets minus your total liabilities from your balance sheet.
- Liquidation Value: This method is used for distressed companies, and its calculations are based on the net asset of a company with fewer assets.
- Market Value: This last method compares a company with its peers and then applies a calculation such as the price-to-earnings ratio (P/E).

Chapter 4

DOCUMENTS

I've talked about the sale documents, but there are others that you should also have ready for the buyer. These documents pertain to your brand's day-to-day operations and offer validation for everything you've said about your brand. So, for example, if you've talked about how your marketing team has done wonders for sales, you will have to turn over any information related to this for the buyer. In this chapter, I will break down the documents into categories, but I would like to mention a few specific things about clients because I believe they are essential to your business.

CLIENT LISTS

Remember, I spoke in a previous chapter about one of the most critical steps once you've decided to sell is that you notify your customers. Of course, many of your customers will have been with you since the beginning, probably showing brand loyalty. But, of course, because you've sold your brand or your dream to someone else, you're hoping they can continue your legacy, and your customers are vital to that. So, rather than see loyal customers move to the competitor, your buyer needs the opportunity to convince them that nothing but the owner of the brand has changed.

Finances

- aging Reports: Accounts Payable and Accounts Receivable
- financial ratios and trends
- statement of discretionary earnings or cash flow
- outstanding loan agreements
- description of liens
- two-three years of tax returns

Business Operations

- business licenses, certifications, and registrations
- professional certificates
- insurance policies
- business plan
- marketing plan with samples of marketing materials
- employment policy manual
- business procedures manual
- photos of business
- organization chart

Product/Services

- inventory list with value detail
- product/Service descriptions with price lists

Clients (Customers) and Suppliers/Distributors

- client list and major client contracts
- supplier and distributor contracts

Brand Specific

- business formation documents
- copies proving ownership of patents, trademarks, and other intellectual property
- any documents unique to your business

Equipment and Building

- list of fixtures, furnishings, and equipment with value detail
- asset depreciation schedule from tax return
- building or office lease
- equipment leases with maintenance agreements

Employees

- staffing list with hire dates and salaries
- employment agreements

Chapter 5

HOW TO SELL

You've decided to sell and now have your business valuation, but how do you sell? What do you do to let potential buyers know your brand is for sale? Most importantly, how do you sell your business discreetly and confidentially?

It's essential to keep the sale of your brand quiet. You don't want to unnecessarily alarm clients, employees, creditors, or investors. And you certainly don't want to let your competitors know you're selling unless you have one in mind to buy your business.

As with everything else, you can take steps to decide who would buy your business and then how you would let them know you have something they might be interested in.

- Decide who or what type of person would be a likely buyer for your business.
- Figure out how to market to these potential buyers.
- Determine advertising strategies.

WORD OF MOUTH

Because you're trying to be discreet, word of mouth is the best form of advertising only when you know for sure that a specific person or business is looking for exactly what you have.

If you have already determined that you'd like to sell to a specific competitor and you know they would be interested, this is where you can get word to them directly or through a connection. Maybe you know of a supplier that has voiced an interest in your business, and further inquiry leads you to believe they've got the financial backing or means to make the purchase. This is another area where word of mouth is the best form of advertising.

Sometimes you have a connection that you were unaware of until you're, for example, at the bank. Your banker comments that they know of a client who's been looking for a company like yours.

But always do your research before spreading the news, even by word of mouth. For example, sometimes, a potential buyer wants to purchase a business, but they don't have the funding available. Therefore, you must ensure that any possible buyers for your business are in a favorable financial position.

BUSINESS BROKER

A business broker knows that a small business's sale must be discreet and confidential. Using a broker as an intermediary is less stressful for you as the seller. You can concentrate on getting your paperwork in order and ensuring that your brand looks as good as it did when you started your business. There are some benefits to using a business broker that may help you decide which way you go when you're ready to sell. Business brokers are:

- experienced: Selling a business is what they do. You can find one that has been in the industry for a while, meaning they will have the appropriate expertise. If you think about it, you'll probably only sell a business once or twice, but business brokers sell many times that in just one year. They can help you price and market your business and give you an unbiased and accurate assessment of your business based on their knowledge of recent sales histories.

- skillful negotiators: Again, this is what business brokers do. They know the ins and outs of negotiating your selling price. Besides, haggling over price can be uncomfortable and frustrating, but a broker can be your representative, giving you the chance to avoid this unpleasant part of selling.
- professional: When searching for a business broker, pay attention to their reputation. You're looking for someone with your best interests at heart because they will take the time to understand your company and how best to market it to potential buyers. In addition, they professionally present information and paperwork to all parties involved in the sale.
- confidential: Since you're trying to keep the sale of your business quiet, the broker who represents you will be able to protect your anonymity. Until the paperwork is signed, you can be assured that you won't go through the difficulties of employees, creditors, investors, or competitors discovering your desire to sell until you're ready.

WEB-BASED BUSINESS SELLER

It is common for individuals and businesses to use the internet to find companies for sale. When you think about that, using an online company to sell your business can feel reasonable. And, of course, their sole aim is to help you sell your business by advertising online. Therefore, I would like to begin this section by pointing out the benefits of using online marketplaces to promote your business for sale.

- nationwide coverage: Advertising online when you're ready to sell your business means you can go further than your community. The online reach is much more extensive than most marketing strategies.
- speed: Your business is instantly available once you've listed it with an online marketplace. When necessary, you can also share documents much faster by selling online.

- insights: You can gain valuable information by tracking data in the online marketplace. You will be able to see how many have visited your listing, etc.
- reviews: You can determine the best platform for listing your business online by reading the reviews of each one.

Using an online company opens many doors because you are not limited geographically. This will be helpful, especially if you don't know who would be the best fit to purchase your brand.

I want to point out that selling your business online requires the same organization and attention to detail that you need when selling through traditional methods.

Also, when you list your business with an online marketplace, you may significantly reduce the risk of word getting out too soon. However, it can also be as private as you need when you use a web-based seller because you can opt to have them provide you with a list of qualified potential buyers rather than advertise in one of the online marketplaces. But if you want to advertise, a web-based company can lead you to the marketplace(s) that will be the best fit for you and your brand.

Chapter 6

GETTING THE WORD OUT

Telling your employees you've sold the business may be the hardest thing to do. They're family, and there will be some panicking once they find out. But there are ways to let them know that will ease their fears and help them understand your decision.

First, don't give out even tidbits or hints before the final sale. There can be adverse effects of telling your employees anything too soon. For example, some long-term employees may not be willing to embrace the idea of working for someone else. Others may even exhibit animosity or poor work performance at the idea of a new owner. And, if the sale takes a while, employees will be left stewing over their future. So here are some tips to make the news palatable and positive for your employees.

Now that I've said not to tell anyone, there may be a few key people you need to let know while you're selling. Your most prominent employees will be the only ones on the "need to know" list. In other words, the employees assisting you in gathering the essential documents needed before, during, and after the sale.

TIMING

Don't let employees learn of the new owner from the internet. Instead, tell them the day after the sale closes to avoid that kind of heartbreak.

Hopefully, you can prevent spreading this news late in the week since it's pretty unpleasant to go into the weekend worrying about the future of your job. The best is to plan an all-staff meeting in the morning to give the news. If you can do it on a Monday, that would be best, as well, because it provides employees all week to ask questions and meet the new owner with you on hand.

TELL IT LIKE IT IS

During the staff meeting, you want to tell your employees what has occurred and give them your reasons. Generally, they will understand. For example, if you're experiencing burnout, let them know. If you need to retire, tell them. Be honest; they've worked for you long enough and deserve honesty. Let them ask their questions but then introduce the new owner and let them field questions, as well. It will help employees if they can see that the new boss is excited to be part of the brand and is willing to answer their questions.

NEXT

A week to absorb the new work situation will be suitable for employees. This time allows them to think about what you've told them. It will be normal for them to discuss it with each other, but you must halt any gossip quickly. Also, encourage the new owner to meet with the employees one-on-one. The new boss can gauge their work ethics and responsibilities from a few minutes of conversation. Finally, since you will still be on site for the week, you can answer any questions the new owner may have, especially after interviews. Getting to know the team will be an essential step for the new owner, and doing it in the comfort of your presence will hopefully offer a smooth transition.

AND THEN

A new owner can offer employees some valuable opportunities, as well. For example, employees can often fall into a rut, never changing how they perform tasks because that's just how it is. But the new boss can sit down and get input on making something work better, or tasks become more streamlined. Letting the employees know their ideas are valuable will help strengthen the new bond between the new owner and the employees.

There is worry all the way around when a business changes hands. The seller worries that the new owner will fire the employees, and the buyer worries that all the employees will quit. However, it is normal for the new owner to recognize the value of the employees they've acquired with their business purchase. The staff is a valuable piece of the business, and the new owner will rely on them to learn the company's ways.

THE LEGAL SIDE OF IT

You will need to discuss the sale with your landlord. You have signed a lease with them, a binding contract, and it is between you and the landlord. So you must work out a contingency plan with the landlord so that the sale paperwork can reflect the new intent with the lease. Anything legal and binding, like a lease, must be addressed upfront during the sale. Therefore, you cannot leave something like that to chance and the hopeful goodwill of your potentially understanding landlord.

In fact, if you have a lease with anyone, including for a piece of equipment, you need to make sure there is a legal plan to transfer the lease to the new owner. I'm sure that it would be easy to forget something like equipment leases when working out the details of a sale, but they are just as legal and binding as a building lease. Remember, strong attention to detail will make the sale of your business run smoother and come out right in the end.

THE CLIENTS MIGHT BE GETTING SUSPICIOUS

Once in a while, a business will use the news they're selling to start a bidding war to get more money. However, that strategy can backfire, and unless you're sure it will work, I don't recommend it.

A general rule of thumb is to tell your clients about the sale once you and the buyer have signed the purchase agreement. Some take that caution one step further and wait until the money is transferred. But there is the possibility that clients and employees who pay attention have noticed something going on, no matter how discreet you are. So rather than letting their worries turn to panic, ease them gently into the new era of your business and let them know you've sold.

In fact, if you're a small business that primarily serves a small community, you can hold an open house. Serve refreshments, pass out goodie bags, and introduce the new owner. Give the clients, distributors, suppliers, the community, and even employees a chance to observe and decide what they think. Chances are, it'll be a case of putting their best foot forward, and your buyer will win them all over. And you can exit the company knowing your legacy will continue.

Chapter 7

PUTTING TAXES IN ORDER

The first thing you need to do before putting your taxes in order is to understand the implications of your sale. You probably have someone do your taxes to avoid making costly mistakes, and you'll have consulted with them before the sale. To put it in perspective, the IRS considers the sale of each asset as an individual piece rather than part of the whole company. So, to really twist the brain cells, your sold assets EACH need to be labeled as:

- inventory
- real property
- depreciable property
- capital assets

Then the gain or loss for each is calculated. The appropriate capital gains tax must be paid, of course.

But it gets stickier. If you decide to keep an ownership stake after the sale, which is common, the taxes get even more confusing. Thank goodness for those tax experts, right? But even if someone else is doing your taxes, figuring out those numbers, you must still know what's going on and your options.

Now comes the intimidating part; making sure you have everything settled and completed with the IRS. If you worry that you may be forgetting something or don't understand a part of the process, the irs.gov website is the place to get your information. The IRS is beneficial, and its website is full of the information you need, along with videos that will walk you through whatever steps you must take to complete the appropriate forms. When you close any business, whether it is:

- Sole Proprietorship: An unincorporated business owned by one individual.
- Partnership: Two or more partners doing business or trade together.
- Corporation: Separate taxpaying entity with even one shareholder—includes S Corporations.

So here's a list of what you must do to settle your taxes. The steps are the same, no matter the type of business. The difference will be some of the forms you'll need. I will at least list the various forms here, also.

FILE FINAL TAXES AND RELATED FORMS

You must file a final tax form for the last year you are in business. So even if you sell in February or November, you were in business for part of that year; therefore, you must file the forms you would typically file for your business type.

Sole Proprietorship

- Schedule C (Form 1040 or 1040 SR)
- Form 4797, Sales of Business Property
- Form 8594, Asset Acquisition Statement
- Schedule SE, Form 1040, Self-Employment Tax, if net earnings are $400 or more.

Partnership

- Form 1065, U.S. Return of Partnership Income

THE PERFECT BRAND JOB

- Check the box that says, "final return," (top of front page below name and address).
- Schedule K-1, partner's Share of Income, Deductions, Credits, Etc.
    - Check the box that says, "final return," (top of front page below name and address).
- Form 4797, Sales of Business Property
- Form 8594, Asset Acquisition Statement

Corporations

- Form 966, Corporate Dissolution or Liquidation
    - Check the box that says, "final return," (top of front page below name and address).
- Form 4797, Sales of Business Property
- Form 8594, Asset Acquisition Statement

C Corporation
- Form 1120, U.S. Corporate Income Tax Return
- Schedule D, Form 1120

S Corporation
- Form 1120-S, U.S. Income Tax Return for an S Corporation
- Schedule D, Form 1120-S
- Schedule K-1, Shareholder's Share of Income, Deductions, Credits, Etc.
    - Check the box that says, "final return," (top of front page below name and address).

DON'T FORGET YOUR EMPLOYEES

Your employees have been faithful and have stuck with you through the ups and downs of getting this brand running smoothly. You don't want to see them punished because you forgot about their part when you completed your year-end paperwork for taxes.

Employment Taxes

- pay final wages and compensations, if any
- make last federal tax deposits
- report employment taxes
    - Form 941, Employer's Quarterly Federal Tax Return **OR**
    - Form 944, Employer's Annual Federal Tax Return
        - Check the box to indicate business closed, enter the date of final wages.
            - Line 17 - Form 941
            - Line 14 - Form 944
        - Attach statement with name and address of individual keeping the records.
    - Form 940, Employer's Annual Federal Unemployment (FUTA) Tax Return
        - Check the box labeled "d" in the Type of Return section—this shows it's the final form.
- Provide W-2, Wage and Tax Statement, copies B, C, and 2
- File Form W-3, Transmittal of Income and Tax Statements to send copy A to the Social Security Administration
- If employees get tips, file Form 8027, Employer's Annual Information Return of Tip Income and Allocated Tips

Pension or Benefit Plans

- If employees receive benefit plans, you must distribute the assets from that plan once it has been canceled. Preferably within a year. Usually, though, the employee can roll over the funds to another qualified program or IRA.
- If a 401K, the employee receives the total vested amount, the combined amount that the employee and employer contributed.
- If you've provided your employees with a Health Savings Account

(HSA) or something similar, you need to read Publication 969, Health Savings Accounts, and Other Tax-Favored Health Plans. In addition, there are a couple of forms you MAY need to file regarding health plans or benefits.
- Form 5329, Additional Taxes on Qualified Plans (Including IRAs) and Other Tax-Favored Accounts
- Form 8889, Health Savings Account (HSAs)

PAY YOUR TAXES

This is the most straightforward step. Once you have completed all the forms, you must pay what you owe.

REPORT PAYMENTS TO CONTRACTORS

If you utilize contractors to do specialty work, you've paid them and need to report those payments.
- Form 1099-NEC, Nonemployee Compensation
- Form 1096, Annual Summary and Transmittal of U.S. Information Returns

CANCEL YOUR EIN, CLOSE YOUR IRS BUSINESS ACCOUNT

The EIN is your Employer Identification Number assigned as your business's permanent federal taxpayer identification number. To cancel and close your IRS account, send a letter with:
- the complete legal name of the business.
- the business EIN.
- the business address.
- your reason for closing the account.

If you still have the notice sent with the EIN when it was assigned, send it with the letter. The account will not be closed until all returns have been filed and owed taxes have been paid.

KEEP YOUR PAPERWORK

The length of time to hold onto your records depends on what kind of records they are.

- property records: Keep any documents relating to the property (business) until the period of limitations expires from when you sold the business.
  - period of limitations: The period of time you have to amend your taxes, or the IRS can assess additional taxes. This length of time can vary depending on various circumstances. You can find the information on the IRS website if you're unsure.
- employment tax records: Keep these records for at least four years.

IN SUMMARY OF YOUR TAXES

Many people find it intimidating to deal with the IRS, but if you file your taxes promptly and pay attention to the forms you're supposed to file, you will be fine. In addition, keeping your records organized and complete during the year will help you when it comes time to file taxes.

Chapter 8

MISTAKES TO AVOID

None of us are perfect, are we? So it's inevitable that we will make mistakes. It would be easy to say, learn from your mistakes, and leave it at that. But that's too easy, too simple of an answer. So yes, the bottom line is that you will have to learn from your mistakes. You probably made one or two while establishing your brand, but you were able to correct those mistakes and create a business that means something. A brand that, once sold to the right buyer, will further establish your legacy. You created something fantastic, didn't you? But each of these mistakes I will list here does not mean the end of the sale. They are not the mistakes you would make at a crucial moment in the selling process. These are mistakes that you can correct before it's too late.

Something to remember while working through the selling process is if you have a partner or spouse, there is more to consider than just your plans when selling the business. You must consider their wishes and remember that they may have input toward the process. Any partner you have will want the same thing you do; to sell the business for the best possible price. To do that, you must ensure that mistakes are kept as lowkey as possible because the cost of fixing the mistakes can eat into your payout.

VALUATION IS TOO HIGH

Maybe you tried it yourself and did what many business owners do when trying to do their valuation. But unfortunately, you priced it too high because you unconsciously put some of the emotion you feel about your brand into your calculations. It's easy to do because, after all, it's your baby, and you created it from the ground floor. There are a couple of ideas about correcting this mistake.

First, if you did your valuation and it's too high, the simplest way to remedy that problem is to hire a specialized person or company to do your valuation. And I can't stress this enough throughout this book, do your research. Remember that a valuation can be skewed one way or the other based on the reason it needs to be done. So research the company that will get the valuation you need to make the right sale.

Now, if a company did the valuation and the valuation is too high, it might be that you used the wrong company. They aren't necessarily a bad company, but the wrong company for you. So again, it comes down to the reason the valuation is necessary. Sometimes, if the professional you hired didn't quite understand what you're looking for or what you need, they may have overreached—just another chance to find someone better.

Because the market will determine your business' value based on supply and demand, the bottom line is that it's worth what someone is willing to pay. Sellers often struggle when they find out their company isn't worth as much as they thought. The blood, sweat, and tears they put into the business should add a hefty markup, right? Unfortunately, it does not. What counts is your brand's performance. So there's a good chance you need to step back and revisit the marketing portion of your exit strategy. I will explain why in just a moment.

But within that valuation may be some missteps with calculations. Your company's SDE, Seller's Discretionary Earnings, must be calculated first. Once the SDE has been decided, the value is determined using a multiple. The same one I talked about in Chapter 3: Determining the Sale Price. I mentioned that the multiple is generally two to four times your SDE and sometimes even two to six times. However, it's between one and three times the SDE for a lower-range market. So maybe you went three times the SDE because, in your eyes, it's worth it.

To fix that? Well, we go back to the exit plan marketing strategy. Suppose your exit marketing strategy proves successful and your company is set for accelerated growth, with the company quality being better than others in the market. In that case, you can get 2 to 2.75 times to be your multiple. So overall, the fix for this mistake is to ensure your business is a proven success that will continue, earning you a higher multiple.

If all else fails, use the Market Value strategy to determine the value of your business. For example, if other companies sell for less than two times their multiple, yours must be exceptional to have a higher value.

TRYING TO DO IT ALONE

Let's face it; none of us are experts at everything. However, I imagine you are an expert at business management, and you've used that skill to grow your brand to the point it's at now. However, you probably don't have experience selling a business. So, if this is indeed your first time selling a business, I cannot strongly recommend enough that you do not do it alone.

Of course, it's tempting to save money during the selling process, but the unforeseen consequences can be costlier than hiring professionals. So naturally, it's also great to have that can-do attitude. You probably figured that since you earned your skills in business management through hard work and determination, there's no reason why the same couldn't apply to selling the business. To some degree, you are correct. But many of the tasks that professionals do during the sale of a company are industry specific. Therefore, they require schooling, degrees, certificates, and years of experience after receiving the education.

- Lawyers
- CPAs
- Business Brokers
- Investment Bankers
- Financial Advisors
- Outsourced CFOs

So you tried to DIY the business selling thing, but it didn't work out, and now you have a mess on your hands. It's time to hire professionals to sweep up the mess and tie up loose ends.

While looking for the professionals you need, you don't want to choose the first one you find. Make an informed choice after:
- asking for referrals from your peers.
- holding a series of interviews for each candidate.
- checking references.

Asking professionals to handle the problems arising from your DIY efforts will cost you. But they can resolve the situation, especially if you've hired someone with top-notch experience and a solid reputation among your associates.

FAILING TO PLAN AHEAD

Forgotten paperwork, missing contracts, an angry landlord, and incomplete financial paperwork are all signs that you did not plan for this day. Remember, I explained that the exit strategy should be in place as soon as the business has been set up. In addition, financial paperwork should be completed promptly and kept up-to-date because you should have them available at a moment's notice.

Unfortunately, this poor planning does not make your business appealing to potential buyers. The value of the business plummets in their eyes because they are suspicious that it's not what they thought it would be. If paperwork isn't completed on time, the automatic assumption is that the company is in trouble. Maybe the buyer is getting a company that is going out rather than growing. These thoughts will go through your buyer's mind and back out of the negotiations.

So you've lost the interested buyer but hope to get another. First, however, this means asking your CPA and lawyer to put in plenty of extra hours to update the financial paperwork and prepare missing documents. Of course, this will cost you, but it's the only plan to put you back on track to sell and move on to the next phase of your life.

INFLEXIBILITY

Sometimes the stress of the selling process can get you down. You're frustrated, and mistakes are made. That frustration grows until you become overwhelmed and begin creating more mistakes.

Sound familiar? We've all been in those situations, and you may find yourself experiencing these feelings at some point while selling your business. First, nothing has been going as planned, and your dreams rapidly fall apart. Then, you wonder why you're even selling the company because it's much more work than anticipated.

Then, exciting news reveals you've got a potential buyer. They're excited because this business is exactly what they are looking for. But, there's a catch; they need seller financing, and you come apart at the seams. You had your heart set on a cash-only sale, and you didn't want to waste your time with financing.

Your first inclination is to refuse and send them on their way. But then, you sit down, take a deep breath, and begin going through your exit strategy folder that you've been holding onto like a lifeline. Then you set up a meeting with your lawyer and CPA, and by the time it's over, you're excited about this prospective buyer, and finally, the end of this selling struggle.

When the struggle has gotten out of hand, and your frustration is so high, it's easy to forget your strategy. The plan you set on paper when you first started the business seems like a lifetime ago, and sometimes it takes stepping back for just a moment to realize that even accepting a condition you weren't hoping for may just give you the sale of your dreams. Better yet, if you recognize that you may be fulfilling someone else's dream, it puts everything in perspective, doesn't it?

YOUR HEART'S NOT IN IT

Sometimes when things get too stressful, it's easy to disengage mentally. However, to keep the process running smoothly and without a hitch, it's best to stay involved throughout the whole thing. You might think that your less-than-interested demeanor will go unnoticed, but that is not the case. Any change of behavior on your part and your employees will notice. In addition, potential buyers will feel the disconnect, putting them off the sale.

I understand it's challenging to appear upbeat constantly, and that isn't what I'm suggesting you do. However, staying involved in the process will keep your mind occupied, hopefully allowing you to remain interested in everything. It's a funny world, but the tiniest hint of a lack of motivation on your part will transfer to the prospective buyer.

Trying to stay motivated will be an encouragement to buyers that they can be successful in the business.

CONCLUSION

A lot of information is packed into this book, and I hope you've come away with a solid plan for your business. There is a lot to absorb in this book, and I hope you've taken it in stages so you can come back for more once you've figured out each step and how it relates to what you're doing with your brand.

I won't go into more detail since I've laid it all out for you, but knowing your *why* is vital to building a solid business that will instill brand loyalty in your target audience. We all want to make a difference in this world, and it's entirely feasible that your business could do just that.

Therefore, here's a list with the steps broken down as a reminder of what you just read.

GROWING YOUR BUSINESS

- Know your *why*.
    - Figure out the problem.
    - Create your solution to the problem.
- Develop a mission statement.
    - Recognize your value and what your brand has to offer.
- Identify your target audience.
    - Niche down.
- Create your unique brand logo.
- Create your brand story.

- Create a purpose statement.
- Develop an actionable plan.
- Introduce yourself.
- Tell your story.
  - Emotionally connect with your target audience.
- Stay authentic and consistent.
- Know your competition.
  - competitive analysis
    - strengths
    - weaknesses
- Communicate with your customers.

SELLING YOUR BUSINESS

- Plan your exit strategy.
  - Research the options.
- Line up your ducks.
  - legal paperwork
  - financial paperwork
  - marketing strategies for the perfect exit plan
- Let the important people know.
- Figure out how much to sell for.
  - professional valuation
  - how to valuate a business
- Documents, so much paperwork!
- How to sell.
  - Have someone in mind.
  - Find a business broker.
  - Sell your business online.
- Spread the news.
  - when to tell
  - how to tell

- who to tell
- Pay your taxes!
- Oh, no, I've made some mistakes. Now what?
    - the valuation is too high.
    - tried to do everything without help.
    - I didn't plan ahead
    - inflexible
    - no motivation

References

A competitive analysis can give your business an edge.|No Boundaries Advisors. (2018, January 17). NBCPA Builders. https://nbcpa.us/the-importance-of-competitive-analysis/#:~:text=Having%20competition%20nipping%20at%20your%20heels%20keeps%20you

Ali, A. (2022, March 8). *Brand voice: 3 steps to success.* Smartbrief. https://corp.smartbrief.com/original/2022/03/brand-voice-3-steps-to-success

Bhasin, H. (2019, January 30). *What is the Importance of a Brand Logo?* Marketing91. https://www.marketing91.com/importance-of-a-brand-logo/

Chris. (2020, April 9). *50+ Tools and Resources to Help You Build a Brand.* Digital Brand Blueprint. https://digitalbrandblueprint.com/50-tools-and-resources-to-help-you-build-a-brand/

Closing a Business | Internal Revenue Service. (2022, March 14). Www.irs.gov. https://www.irs.gov/businesses/small-business-self-employed/closing-a-business

Cordova, J. (2021, April 28). *The Top Mergers and Acquisitions Benefits You Should Know.* Windes. https://windes.com/the-top=mergers-and-acquisitions-beneftis-you-should-know

Couchman, H. (2017, October 5). *What's The Purpose Of Brand Purpose? Everything You Need To Know.* Fabrickbrands.com. https://fabrickbrands.com/whats-the-purpose-of-brand-purpose/

Council, F.C. (2017, August 30). *Council Post: 12 Ways To Communicate Your Brand To Customers For Increased Recognition.* Forbes. https://www.forbes.com/sites/forbescommunicationcouncil/2017/08/30/12-ways-to-communicate-your-brand-to-customers-for-increased-recognition/?sh=4cc4f1521b5f

Cvetkovic, A. (2021, December 17). *How to Build a Brand Story: Lessons from Retail Branding Experts.* Shopify. https://www.shopify.com/retail/brand-story

Fernando, J. (2021, March 1). *Initial Public Offering - IPO Definition.* Investopedia. https://www.investopedia.com/terms/i/ipo.asp

Gans, D. (2022, August 25). *Selling My Business Online: How to Use Baton to Prepare And Sell.* Baton Market. https://learn.batonmarket.com/selling-my-business-online/

Habib, May. (2022, April 26). *3 reasons why brand consistency matters.* Smartbrief. https://corp.smartbrief.com/orignial/2022/04/3-reasons-why-brand-consistency-matters

Hall, J. (2017, June 18). *5 Ways To Maintain Brand Consistency As You Grow Your Business.* Forbes. https://www.forbes.com/sites/johnhall/2017/06/18/5-ways-to-maintain-brand-consistency-as-you-grow-your-business/?sh=47d7d50561f3

Handelsman, M. (2012, April 25). *Selling Your Business? Get Your Documents in Order.* Inc.com. https://www.inc.com/mike-handelsman/selling-your-business-get-your-documents-in-order.html

Handelsman, M. (2012b, May 30). *How to Market Your Business for Sale.* Inc.com. https://www.inc.com/mike-handelsman/how-to-market-your-business-for-sale.html#:~:text=If%20you%20know%20a%20specific%20person%20or%20business

Heaslip, E. (2021, August 20). *What is a Business Valuation and How Do You Calculate It?* Https://Www.uschamber.com/Co. https://www.uschamber.com/co/run/finance/how-to-calculate-business-valuation

Hill, K. (2021, December 16). *20+ Mistakes to Avoid when Selling Your Business.* Preferred CFO. https://preferredcfo.com/20-mistakes-to-avoid-when-selling-your-business/

Houraghan, S. (2019, November 12). *BRAND PURPOSE: The Definitive Guide (21 Best Examples).* Brand Master Academy. https://brandmasteracadmy.com/brand-purpose/

How Much Can I Sell My Business For?|Valuation|Transworld. (n.d.). Www.tworld.com. Retrieved September 4, 2022, from https://www.tworld.com/sell-a-business/seller-faq/how-much-can-I-sell-my-business-for/?cn-reloaded=1

How to Define Your Purpose, Vision, Mission, Values, and Key Measures. (2016, February 25). NOBL Academy. https://academy.nobl.io/how-to-define-your-purpose-vision-mission-values-and-key-measures/

https://www.facebook.com/thebalance.com. (2019). *3 Ways to Discover What Your Small Business Is Really Worth.* The Balance. https://www.thebalance.com/business-valuation-methods-2948478

https://www.facebook.com/thebalance.com. (2019b). *5 Mistakes to Avoid When Selling Your Small Business.* The Balance Small Business. https://www.thebalancesmb.com/selling-your-small-business-mistakes-2890127

Javed, F. (2020, August 13). *Brand Essentials - How to Create an Authentic Brand Story.* Chimpist. https://www.chimpist.com/essential-tips-to-create-an-authentic-brand-story/

Lake, L. (2019, November 30). *What is Your "Targete Audience" in Marketing?* The Balancce Small Business; The Balance. https://www.thebalancesmb.com/what-is-a-target-audience-2295567

Marion. (2016, June 30). *Finding Your Brand Purpose: What Do You Stand For?* The Branding Journal. https://www.thebrandingjournal.com/2016/06/brand-purpose/#:~:text=To%20find%20your%20brand%20purpose%20you%20need%20to

Nick. (2021, April 9). *The Power of Niching Down|Why Should You Niche Down? -* NINE-FIVE TO FREEDOM. Nine Five to Freedom. https://ninefivetofreedom.com/niche-down/

Offerdahl, J. (2016, May 11). *"How do I tell my employees I've sold the business?"* Www.linkedin.com. https://www.linkedin.com/pulse/how-do-i-tell-my-employees-ive-sold-business-jay-offerdahl/

Pace, K. (2020, May 25). *StoryBrand to grow your business.* StoryBrand to Grow Your Business|Words for Wellness. https://www.wordsforwellness.com/blog/post/53207/StoryBrand-to-grow-your-business/

Pace, K. (2022, February 28). *What problem does your product or service solve?* What Problem Does Your Product or Service Solve?|Words for Wellness. https://www.wordsforwellness.com/blog/post/77454/what-problem-does-your-product-or-service-solve/

Pascarella, S. (2019, October 23). *Exit Strategies & Legal Agreements.* Pascarella & Gill PC. https://www.pasgillcpa.com/exit-strategies-legal-agreements/

Peek S. (2019, March 7). *How to Develop an Exit Plan for Your Business.* Https://Www.uschamber.com/Co. https://www.uschamber.com/co/start/strategy/business-exit-plan

Prins, N. (2021, February 20). *How To Prepare your Business Exit Strategy.* IBrandStudio. https://ibrandstudio.com/articles/how-to-prepare-business-exit-strategy#:~:text=Along%20with%20financial%20 statements%202C%20business%20documentatio%20is%20 something

Sinek, S. (2009, September). *How great leaders inspire action.* Ted.com; TED Talks. https://www.ted.com/talks/simon_sinek_how_great_leaders_ inspire_action?language=en

Team, U. (2021, November 3). *What Is a Mission Statement? Basics and Examples for 2022|Upwork.* Upwork.com. https://www.upwork.com/ resources/mission-statement

Tiffany. (2018, April 25). *What is a Business Brand? Your Answer Revealed…* How to Entrepreneur. https://howtoentrepreneur.com/what-is-a-business-brand

Wertsch, K. (2021, June 1). *How to Find Your Brand Voice.* Engaged Digital Marketing. https://engagedmarketingcompany.com/how-to-find-your-brand-voice/

What is an IPO Exit Route strategy? - Upstox. Upstox.com. https://upstox.com/ learning-center/ipo/what-is-an-ipo-exit-route/

Williamson, P. (n.d.). *How to sell my business online.* Selling My Business. Retrieved September 4, 2022, from https://www.sellingmybusiness. co.uk/articles/selling/how-to-sell-my-business-online

YEC. (2021, November 29). *Council Post: Your Exit Strategy: Five Marketing Strategies To Maximize Valuation.* Forbes. https://www.forbes.com/ sites/theyec/2021/11/29/your-exit-strategy-five-marketing-strategies-to-maximize-valuation/?she=4f995f21606f

Check Out Another Great Book From Baldega Books!

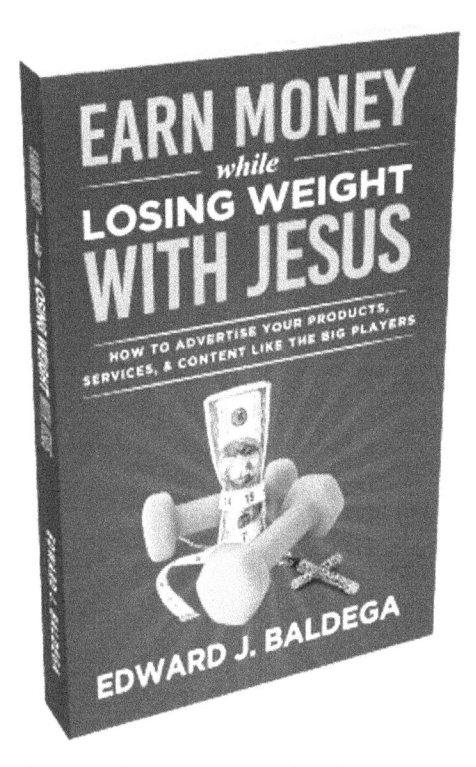

It can be tough to know where to start when it comes to advertising your content. You don't want to waste time and money on strategies that don't work.

Earn Money While Losing Weight With Jesus: How to Advertise Your Products, Services, & Content Like the Big Players is here to help!

This book breaks down advertising for you by category and provides helpful tips on how to make the most of your advertising budget.

Learn from the best in the business – *Dissect, analyze, and utilize those same strategies to get amazing results!*

CPSIA information can be obtained
at www.ICGtesting.com
Printed in the USA
LVHW081242281022
731594LV00011B/1207

9 781959 209034